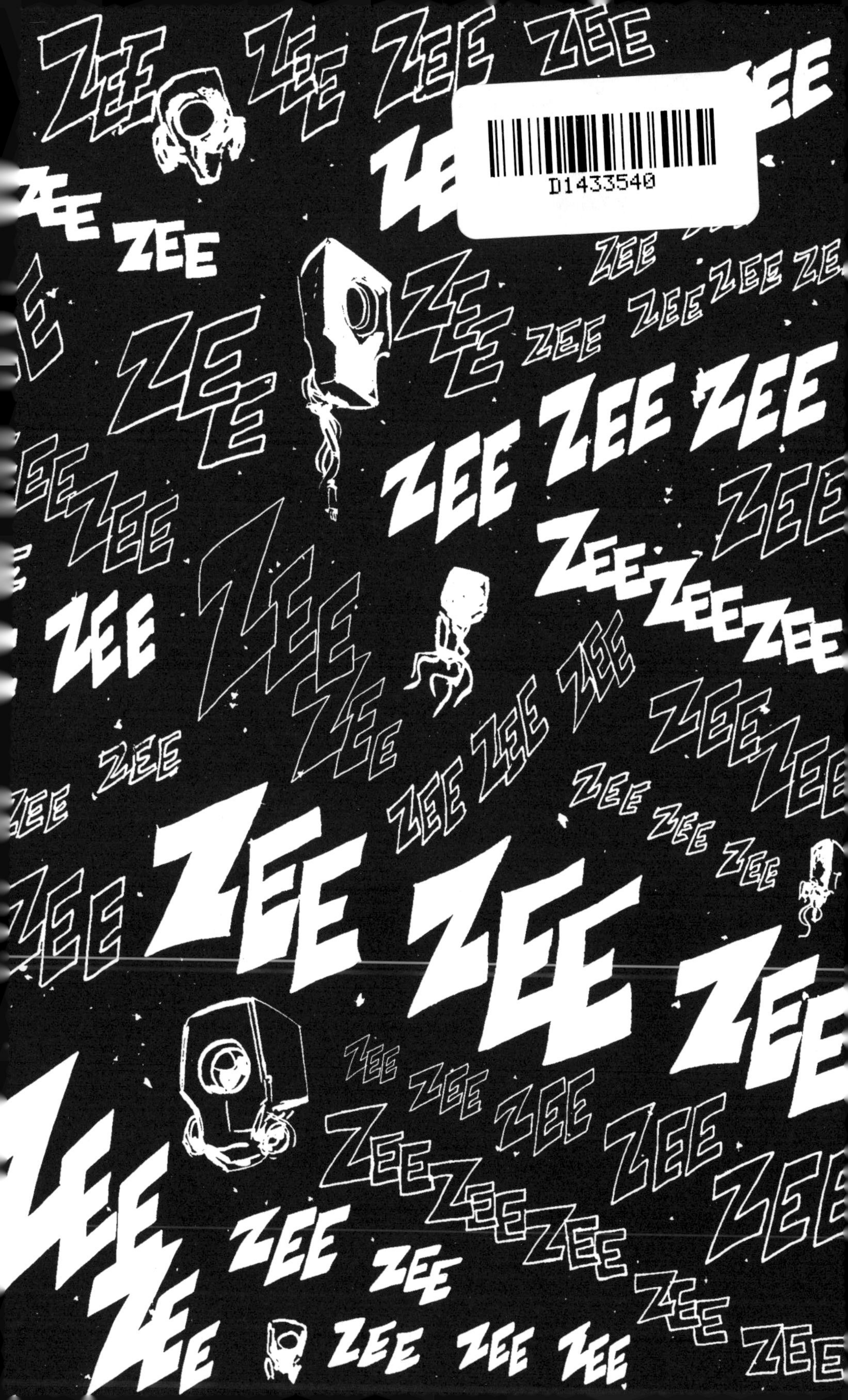
ZEE ZEE ZEE ZEE
ZEE ZEE ZEE ZEE ZEE
ZEE ZEE ZEE ZEE
ZEE ZEE ZEE ZEE ZEE

DEGA

Dan McDaid

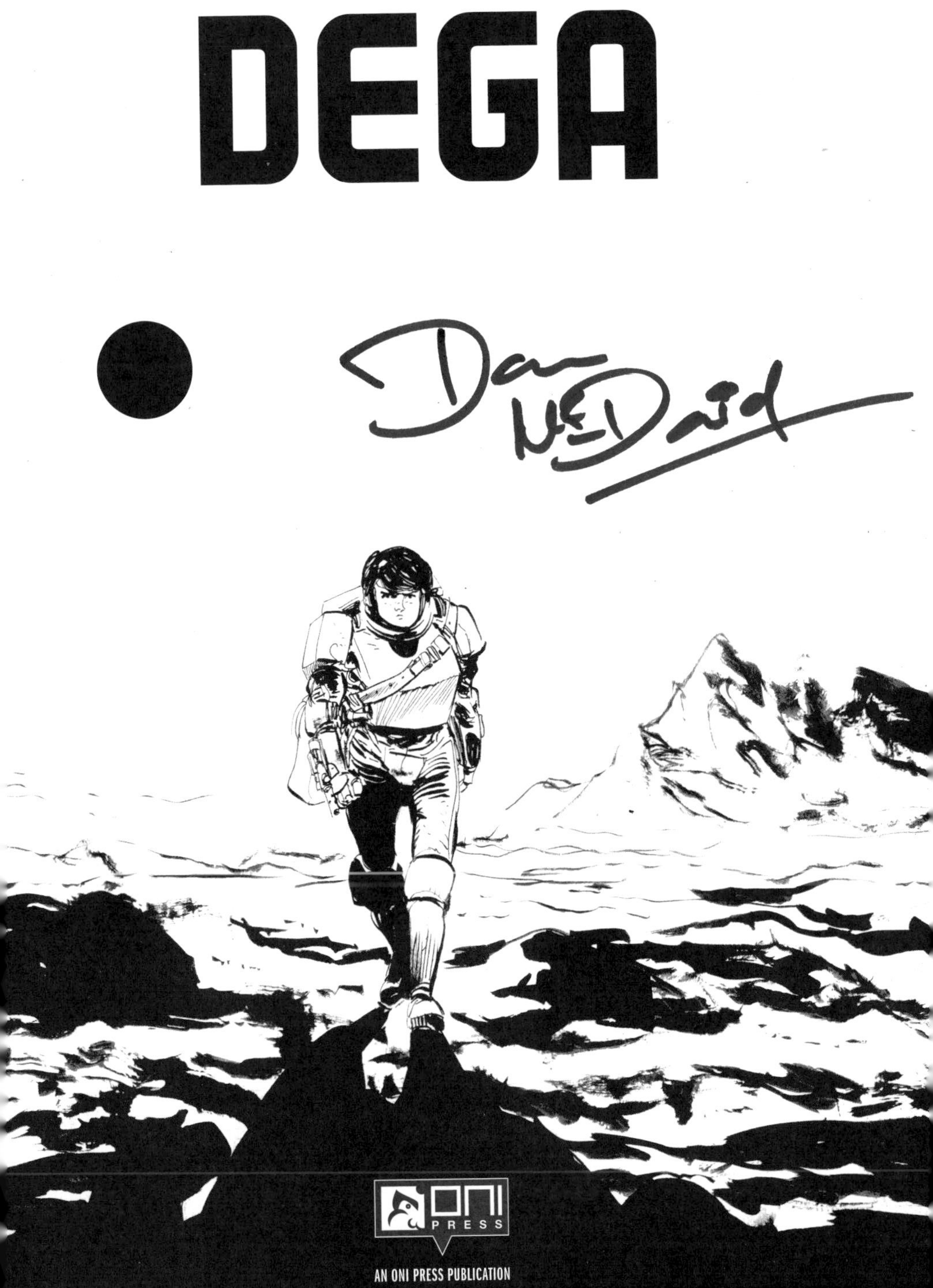

AN ONI PRESS PUBLICATION

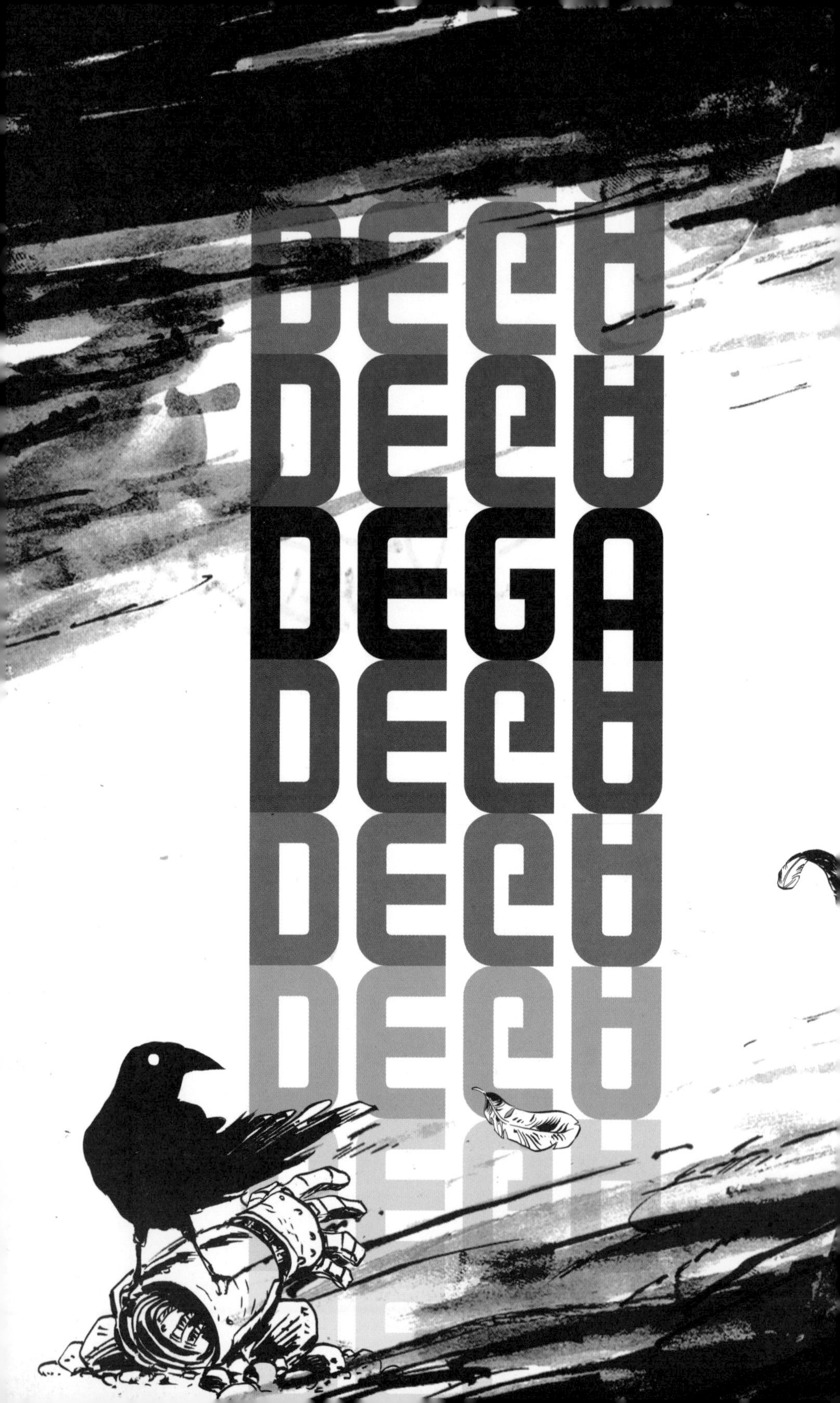
DEGA

Written and Illustrated by

DAN MCDAID

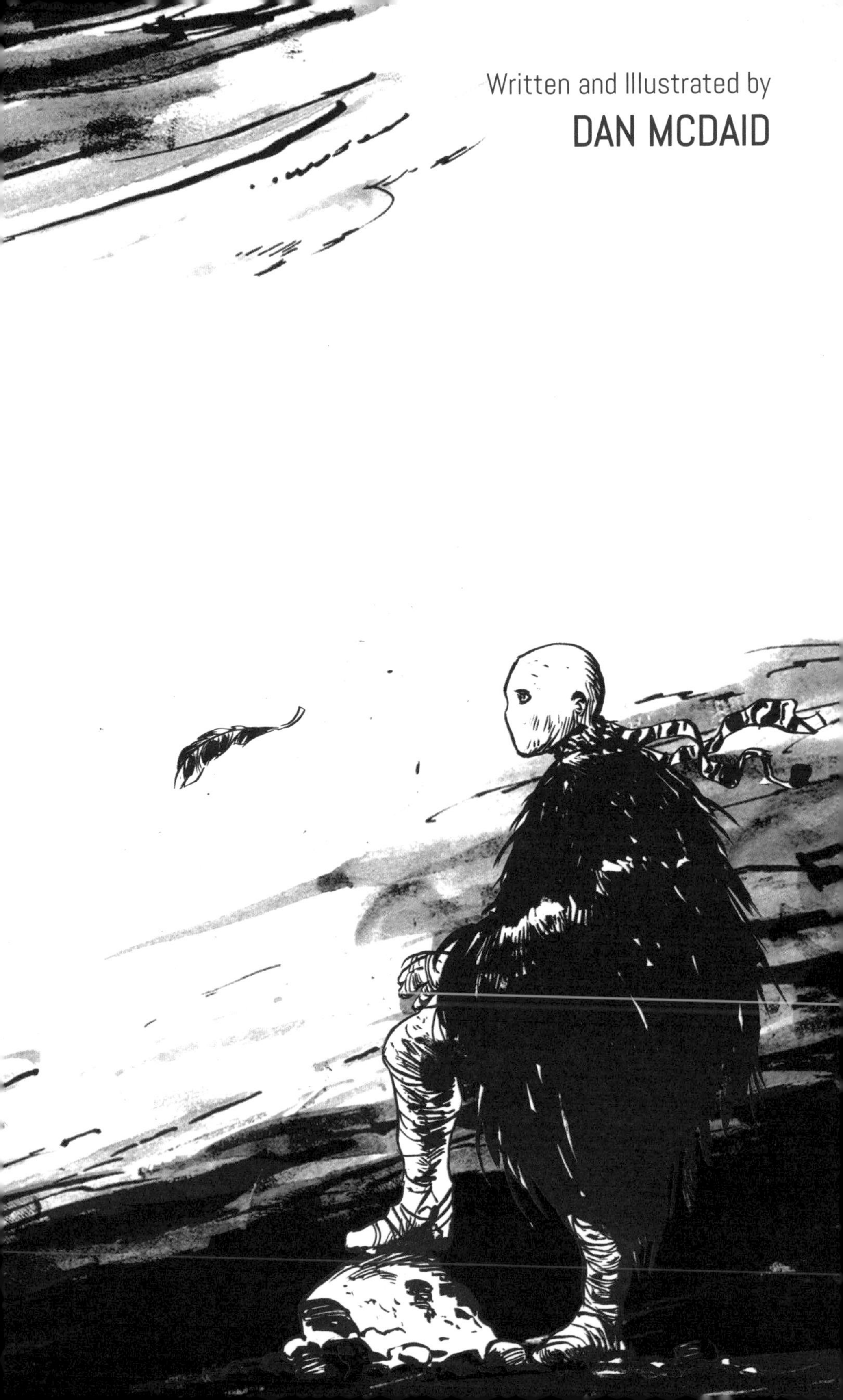

PUBLISHED BY ONI-LION FORGE PUBLISHING GROUP, LLC.

Steve Ellis, e.v.p. of games & operations
Michelle Nguyen, associate publisher
Brad Rooks, director of operations
Katie Sainz, director of marketing
Tara Lehmann, publicity director
Holly Aitchison, consumer marketing manager
Troy Look, director of design & production
Angie Knowles, production manager
Sarah Rockwell, graphic designer
Carey Soucy, graphic designer
Hilary Thompson, graphic designer
Vincent Kukua, digital prepress technician
Chris Cerasi, managing editor
Bess Pallares, editor
Desiree Rodriguez, editor
Grace Scheipeter, editor
Zack Soto, editor
Gabriel Granillo, editorial assistant
Ben Eisner, game developer
Sara Harding, entertainment executive assistant
Jung Lee, logistics coordinator
Kuian Kellum, warehouse assistant

Joe Nozemack, publisher emeritus

@danmcdaid | @danmcdaidart | onipress.com

First Edition: January 2023
ISBN: 978-1-63715-196-9
eISBN: 978-1-63715-854-8

Printing numbers:
10 9 8 7 6 5 4 3 2 1

Library of Congress Control Number:
2022939134

DEGA VOL. 1, January 2023. Published by Oni-Lion Forge Publishing Group, LLC., 1319 SE Martin Luther King Jr. Blvd., Suite 240, Portland, OR 97214.

Printed in China.

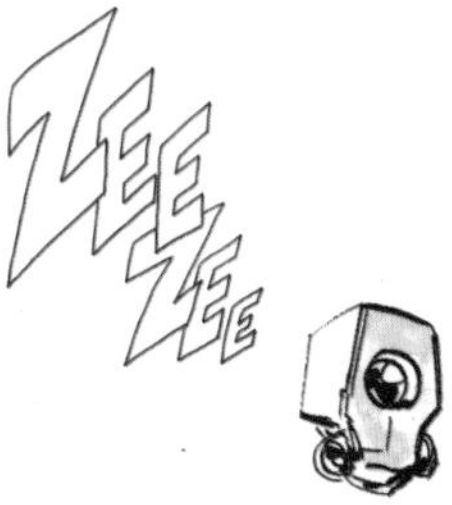
ZEE ZEE

Written and Illustrated by
DAN MCDAID
Original edition designed by
DAN MCDAID
Oni Press edition designed by
SARAH ROCKWELL
Edited by
GABRIEL GRANILLO

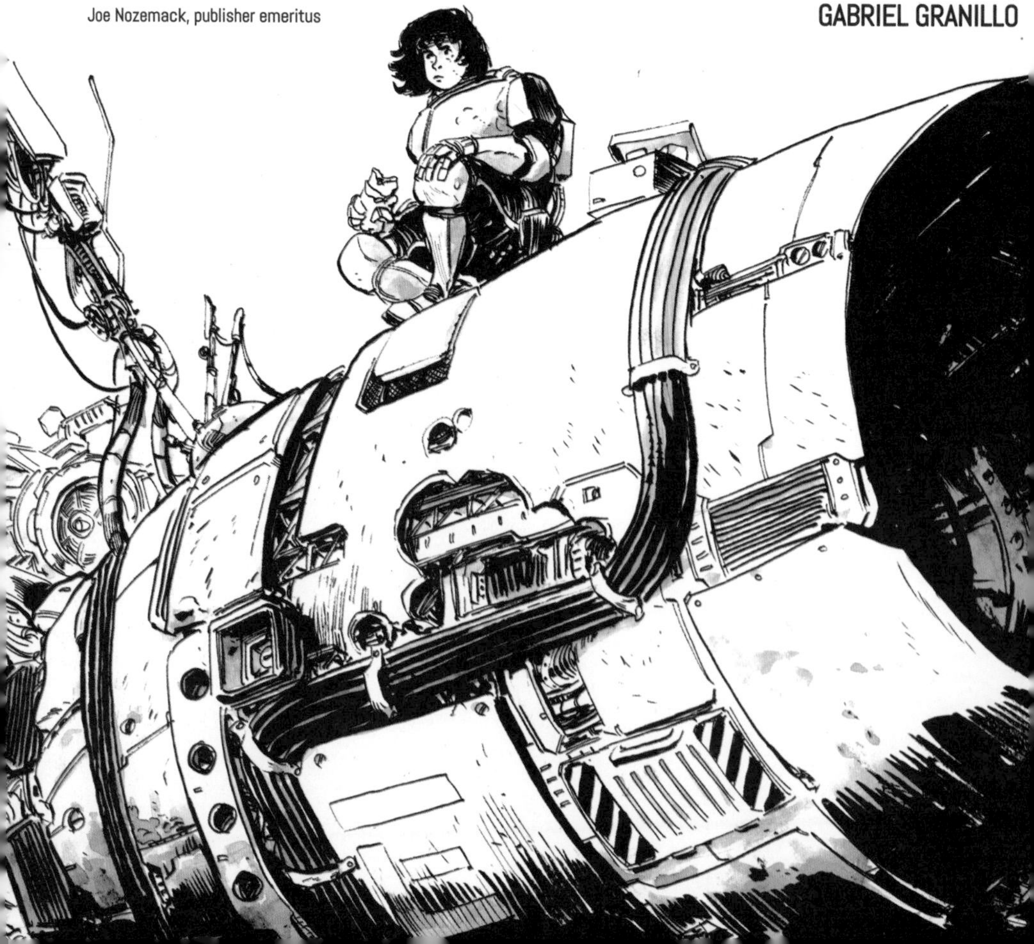

For Deborah

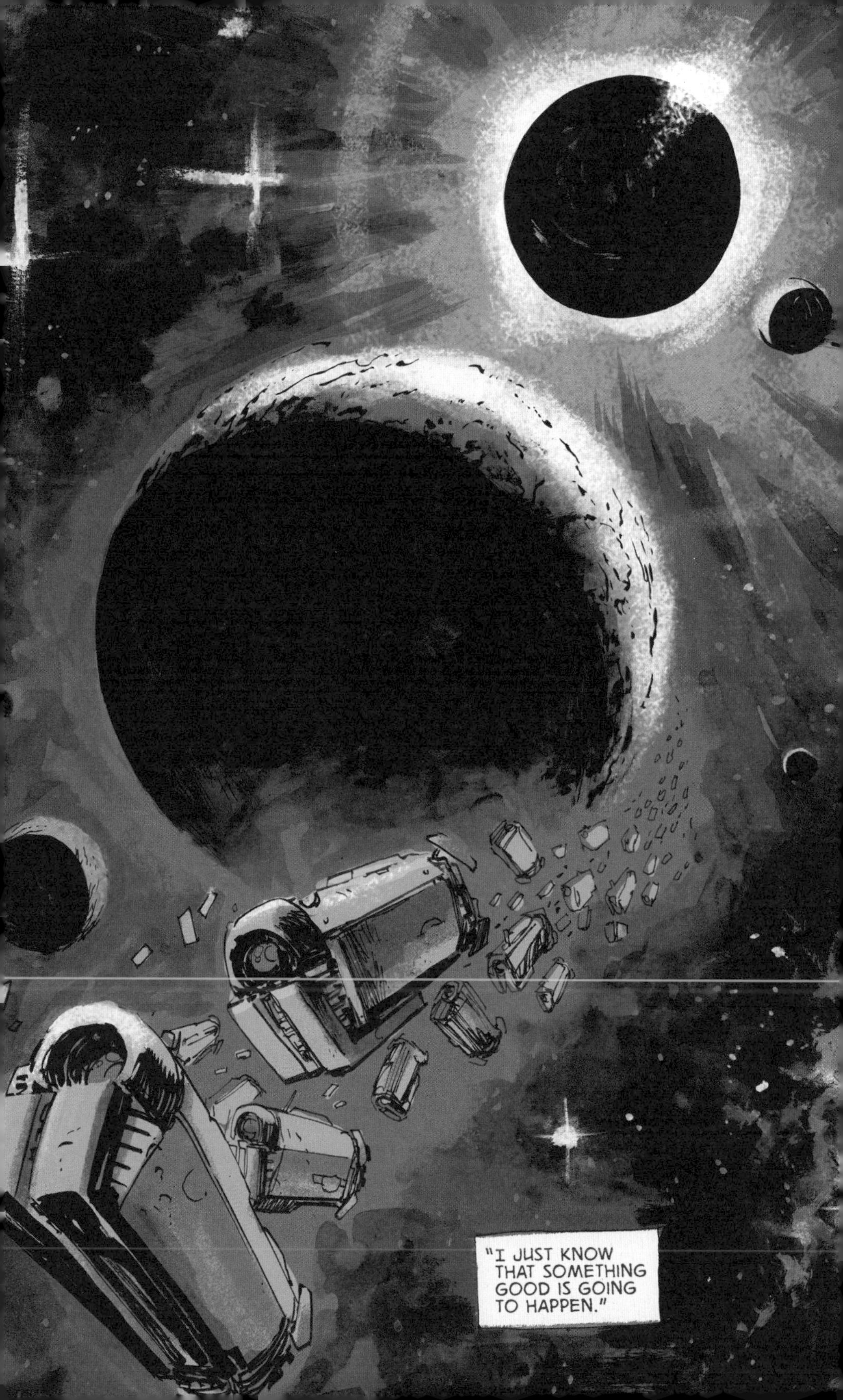
"I JUST KNOW THAT SOMETHING GOOD IS GOING TO HAPPEN."

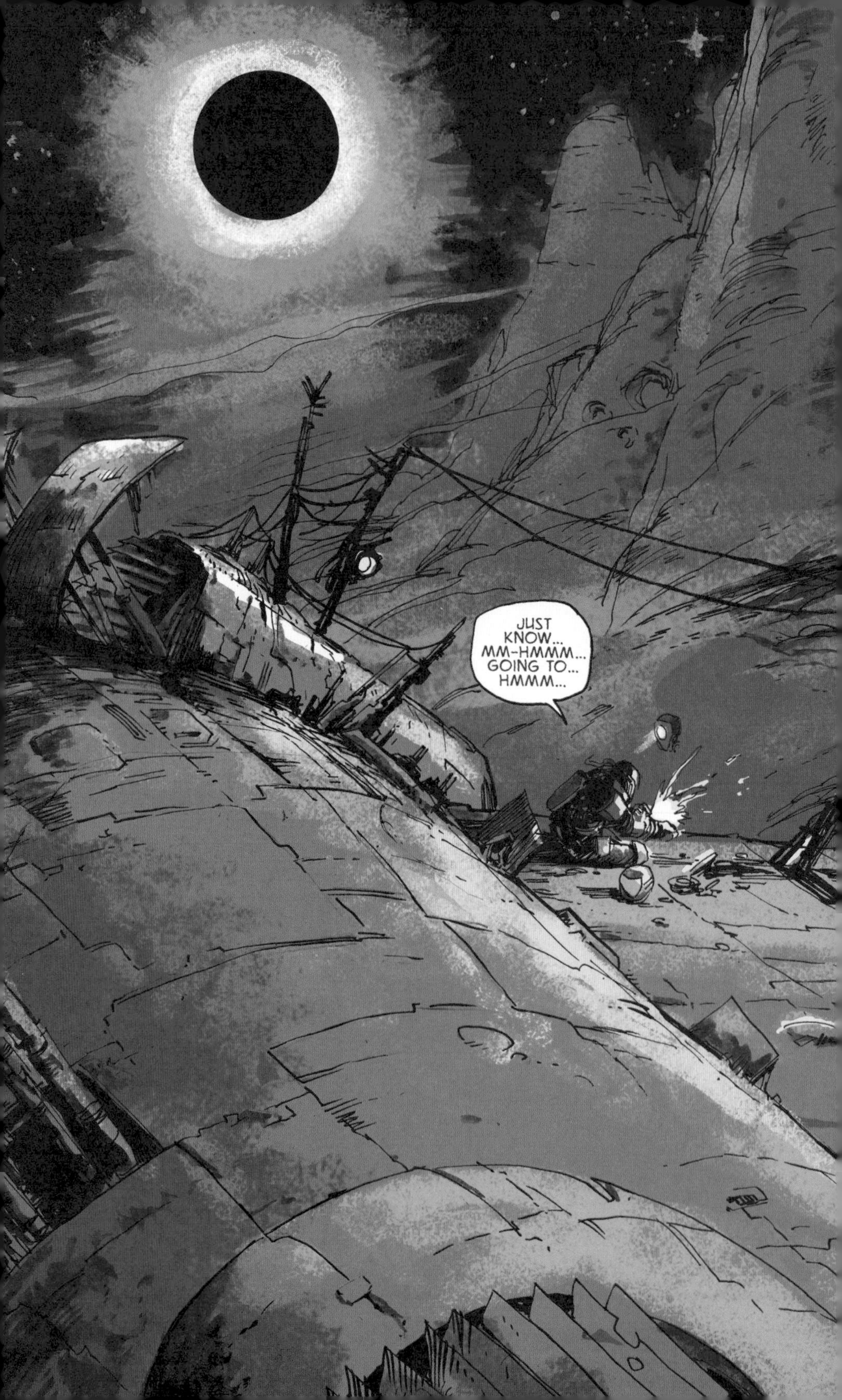
JUST KNOW... MM-HMMM... GOING TO... HMMM...

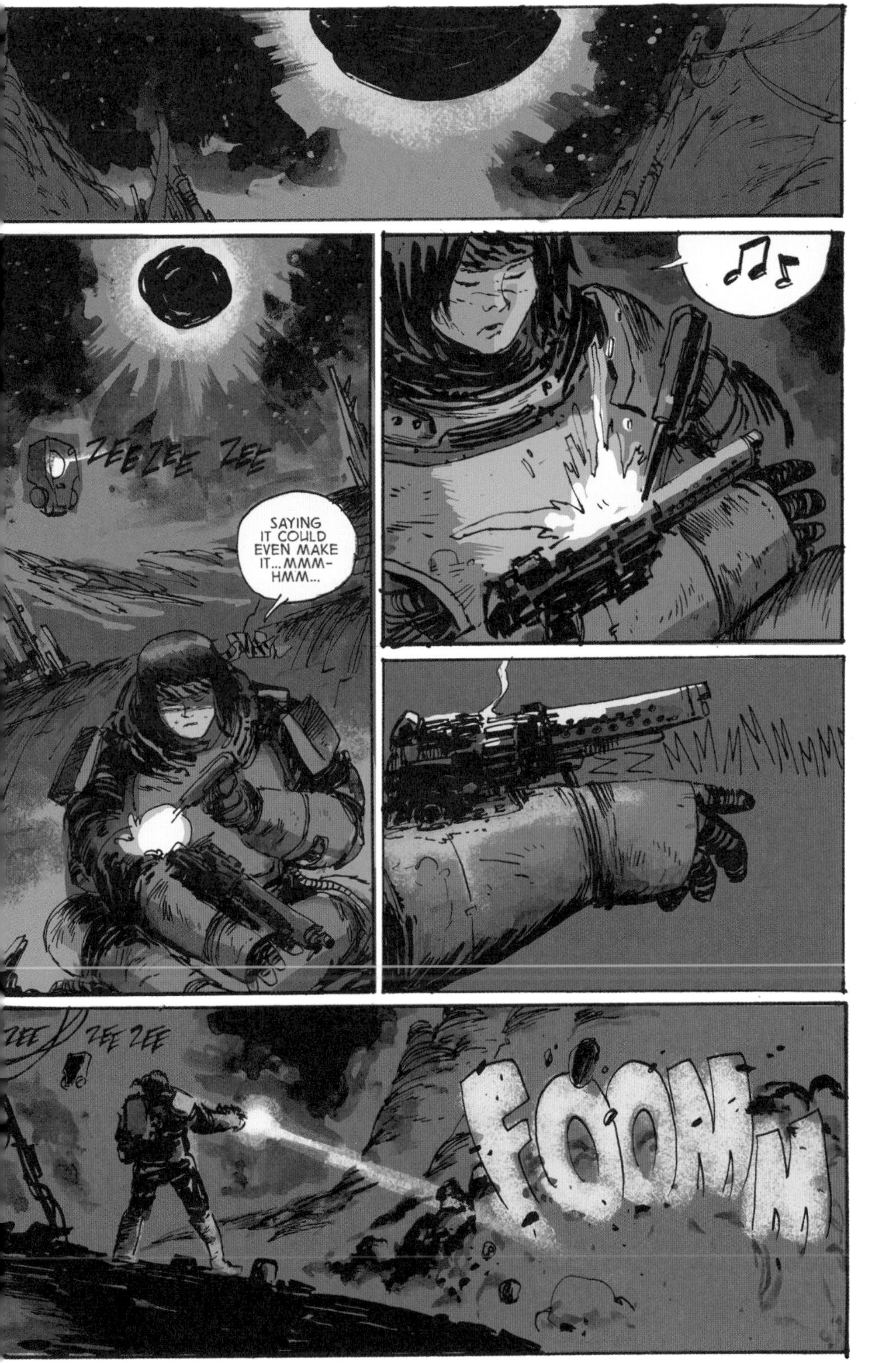

ZEE ZEE ZEE
SAYING IT COULD EVEN MAKE IT... MMM-HMM...
ZEE ZEE ZEE
FOOMM

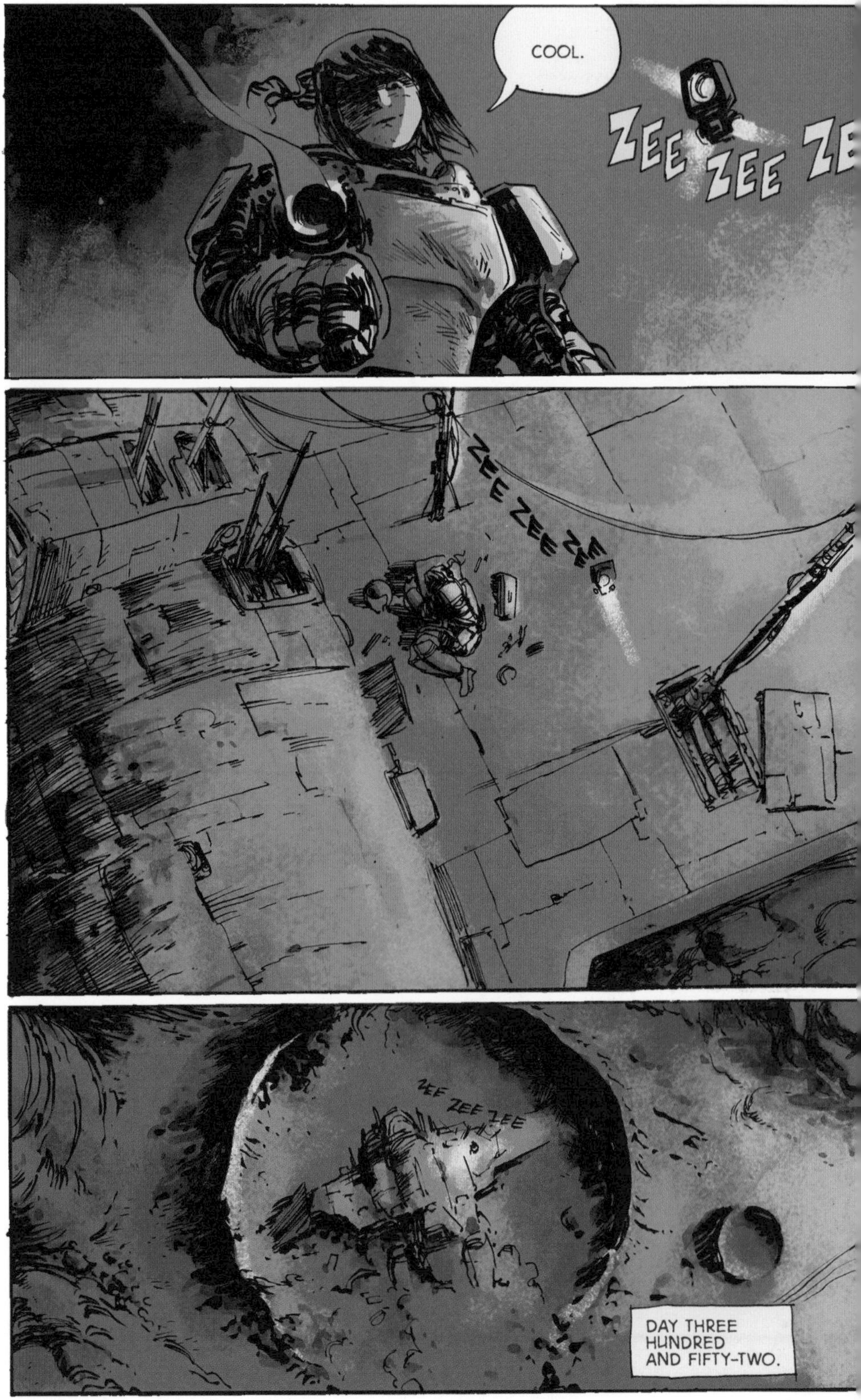
COOL.
ZEE ZEE ZE
ZEE ZEE ZEE
ZEE ZEE ZEE
DAY THREE HUNDRED AND FIFTY-TWO.

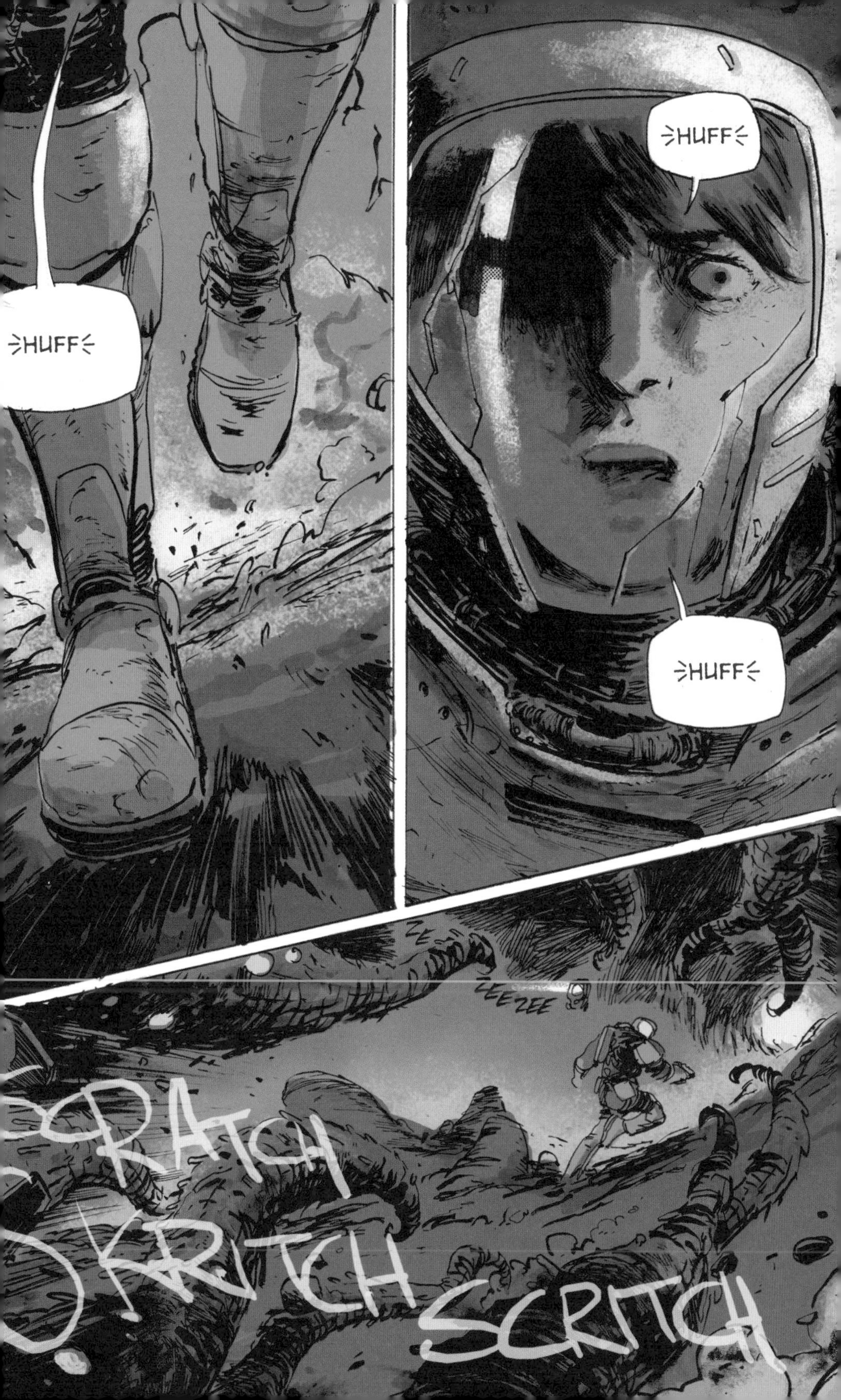
HUFF
HUFF
HUFF
ZEE ZEE
SCRATCH
SKRITCH
SCRITCH

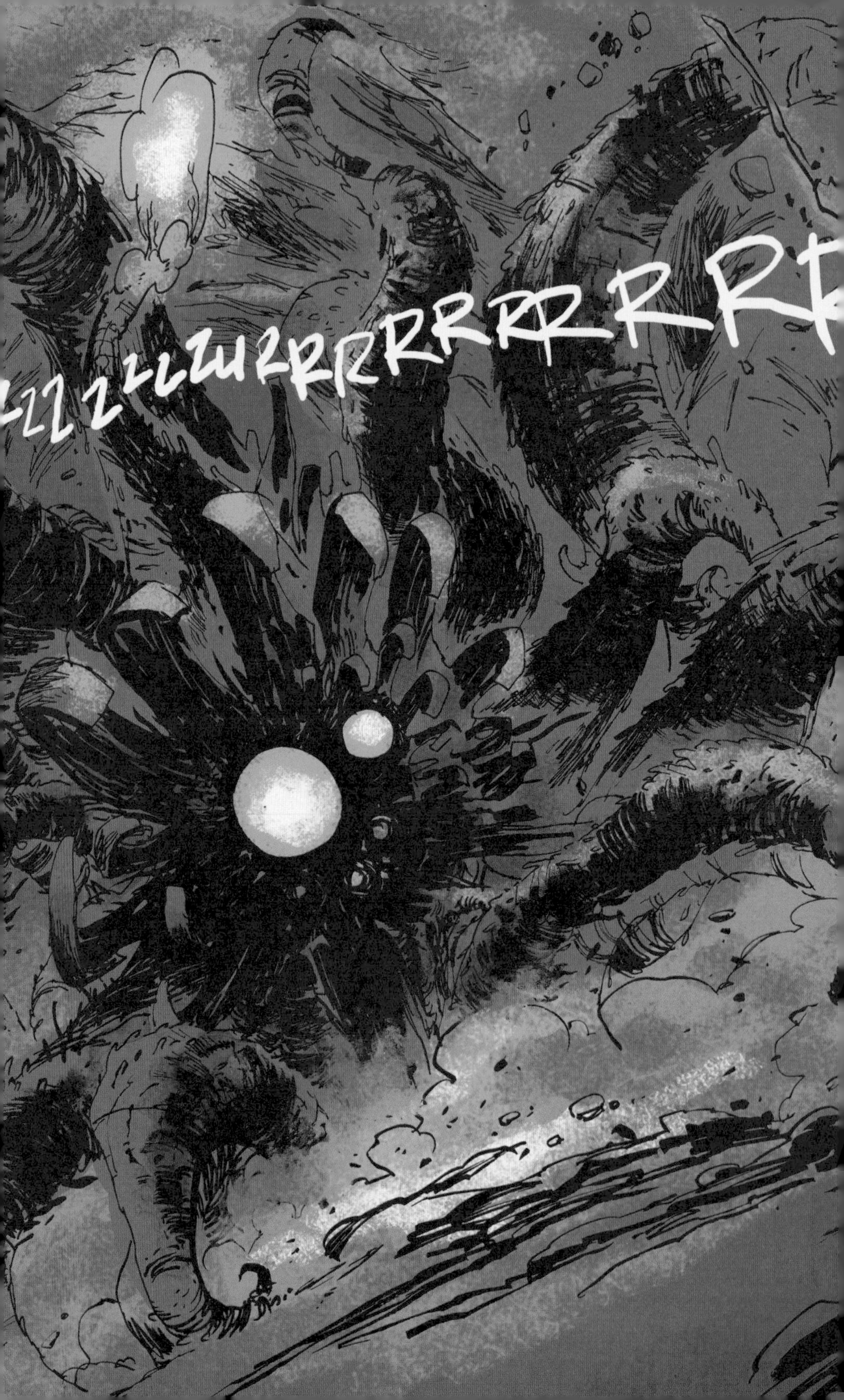
ZZZZZZZZURRRRRRRRRRR

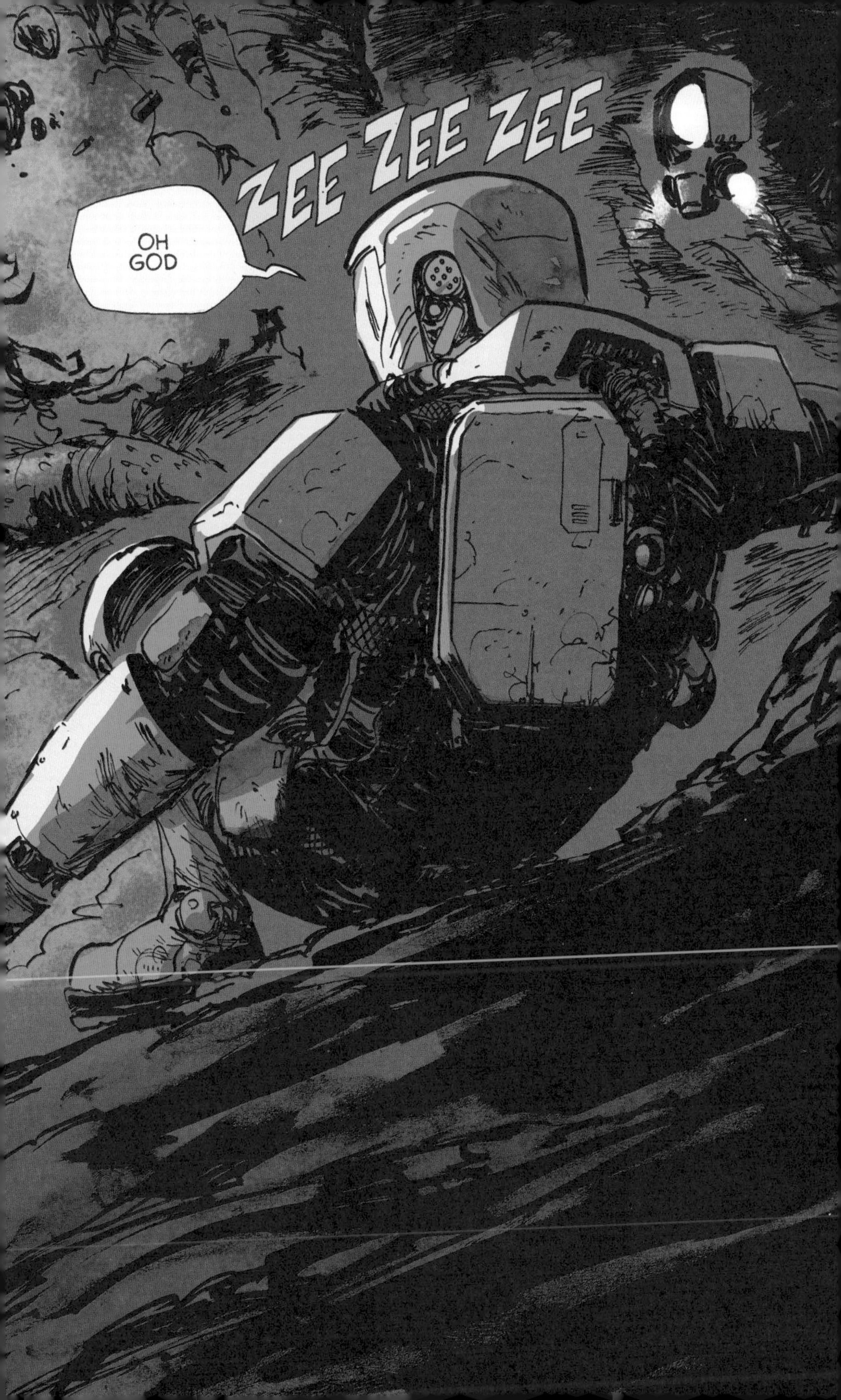
OH GOD
ZEE ZEE ZEE

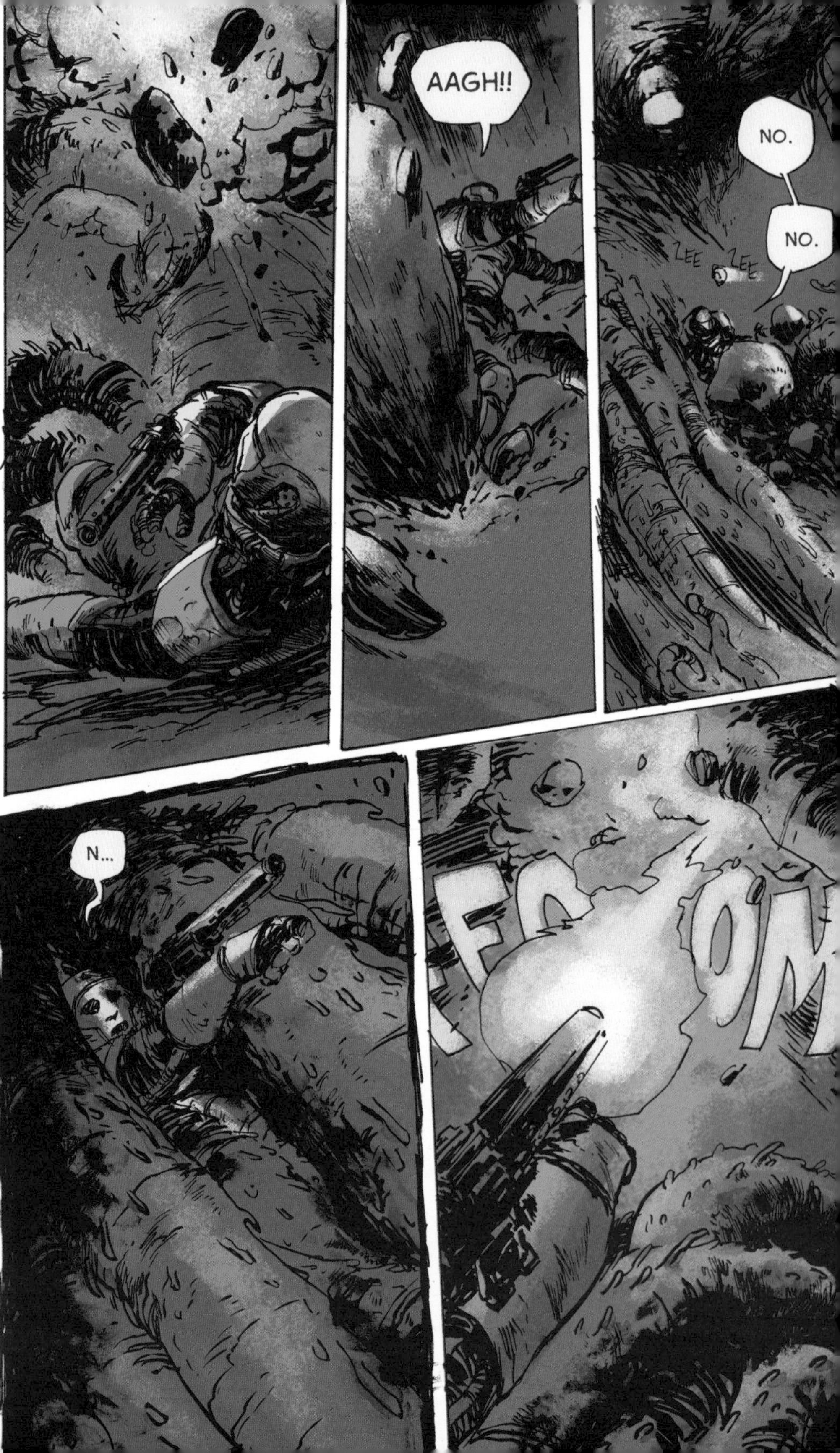
AAGH!!
NO.
NO.
ZEE ZEE
N...

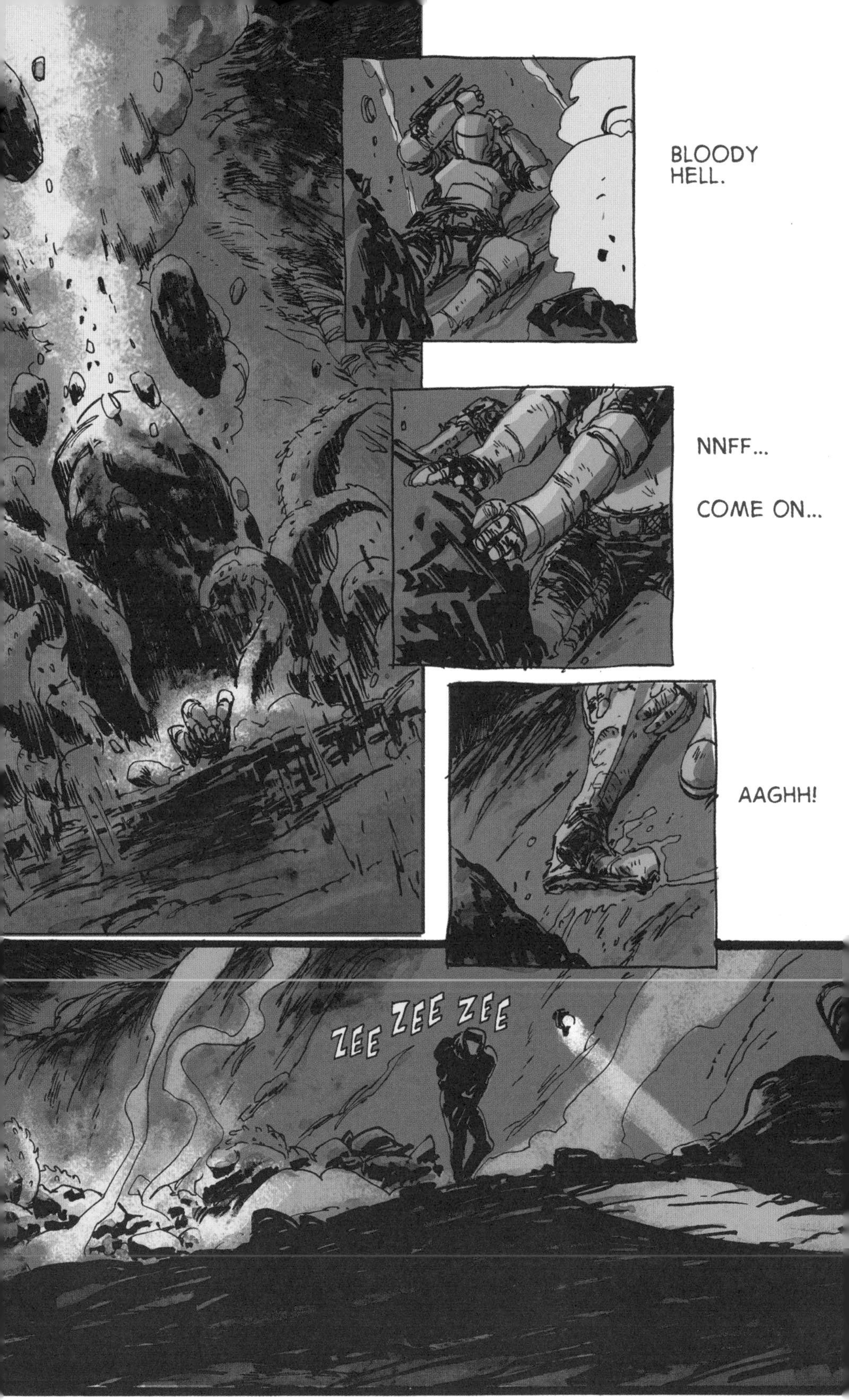
BLOODY HELL.
NNFF...
COME ON...
AAGHH!
ZEE ZEE ZEE

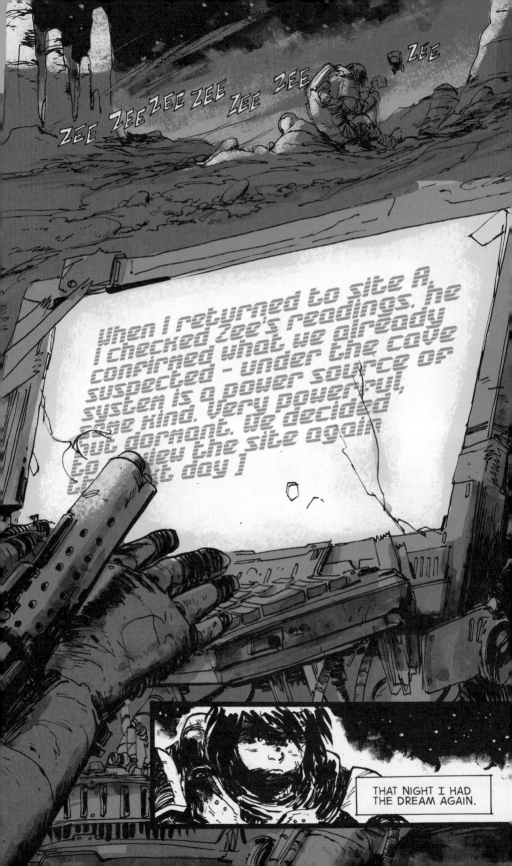

ZEE ZEE ZEE ZEE ZEE ZEE ZEE

When I returned to site A, I checked Zee's readings. he confirmed what we already suspected – under the cave system is a power source of some kind. Very powerful, but dormant. We decided to survey the site again next day]

THAT NIGHT I HAD THE DREAM AGAIN.

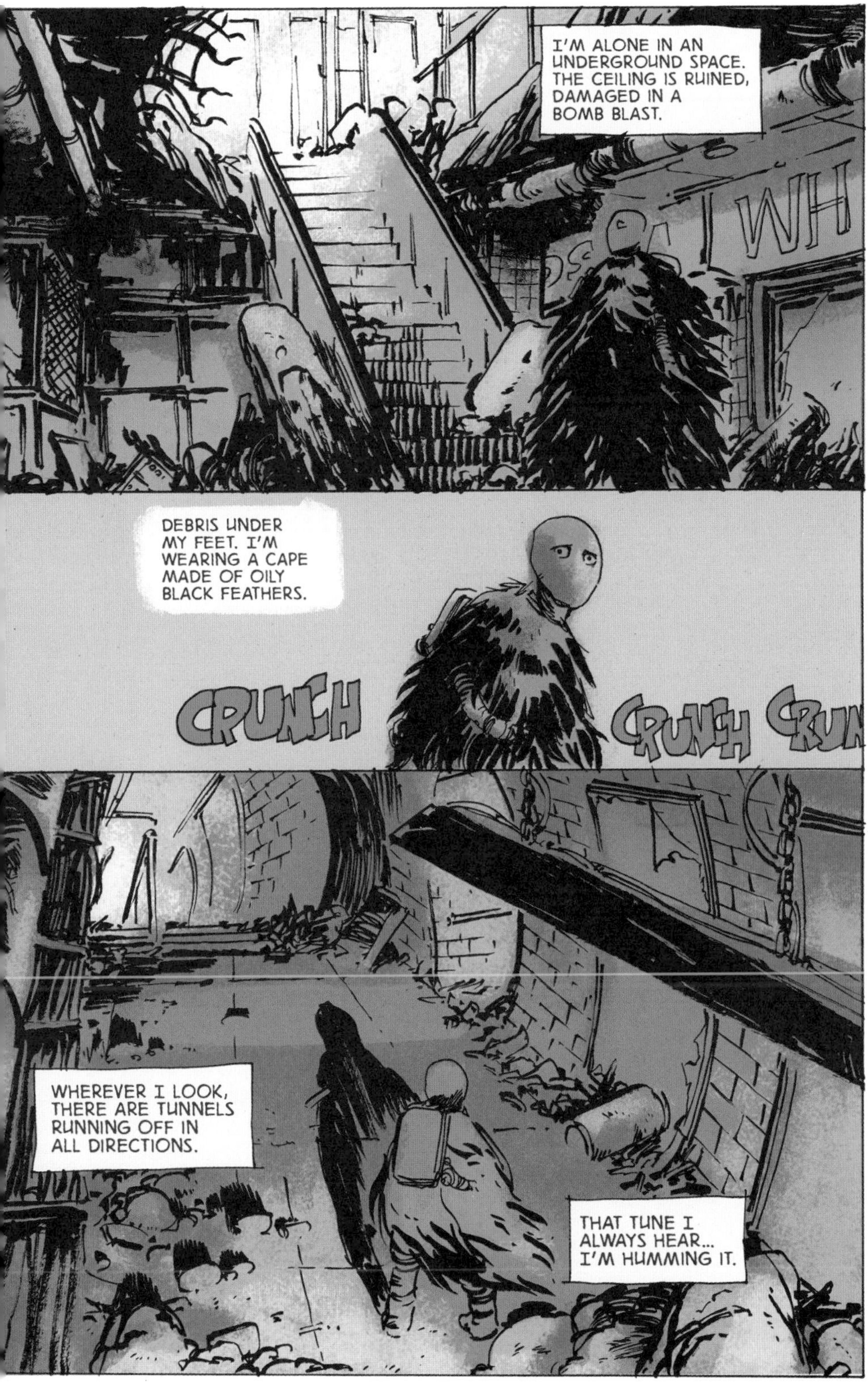
I'M ALONE IN AN UNDERGROUND SPACE. THE CEILING IS RUINED, DAMAGED IN A BOMB BLAST.
DEBRIS UNDER MY FEET. I'M WEARING A CAPE MADE OF OILY BLACK FEATHERS.
CRUNCH
CRUNCH
WHEREVER I LOOK, THERE ARE TUNNELS RUNNING OFF IN ALL DIRECTIONS.
THAT TUNE I ALWAYS HEAR... I'M HUMMING IT.

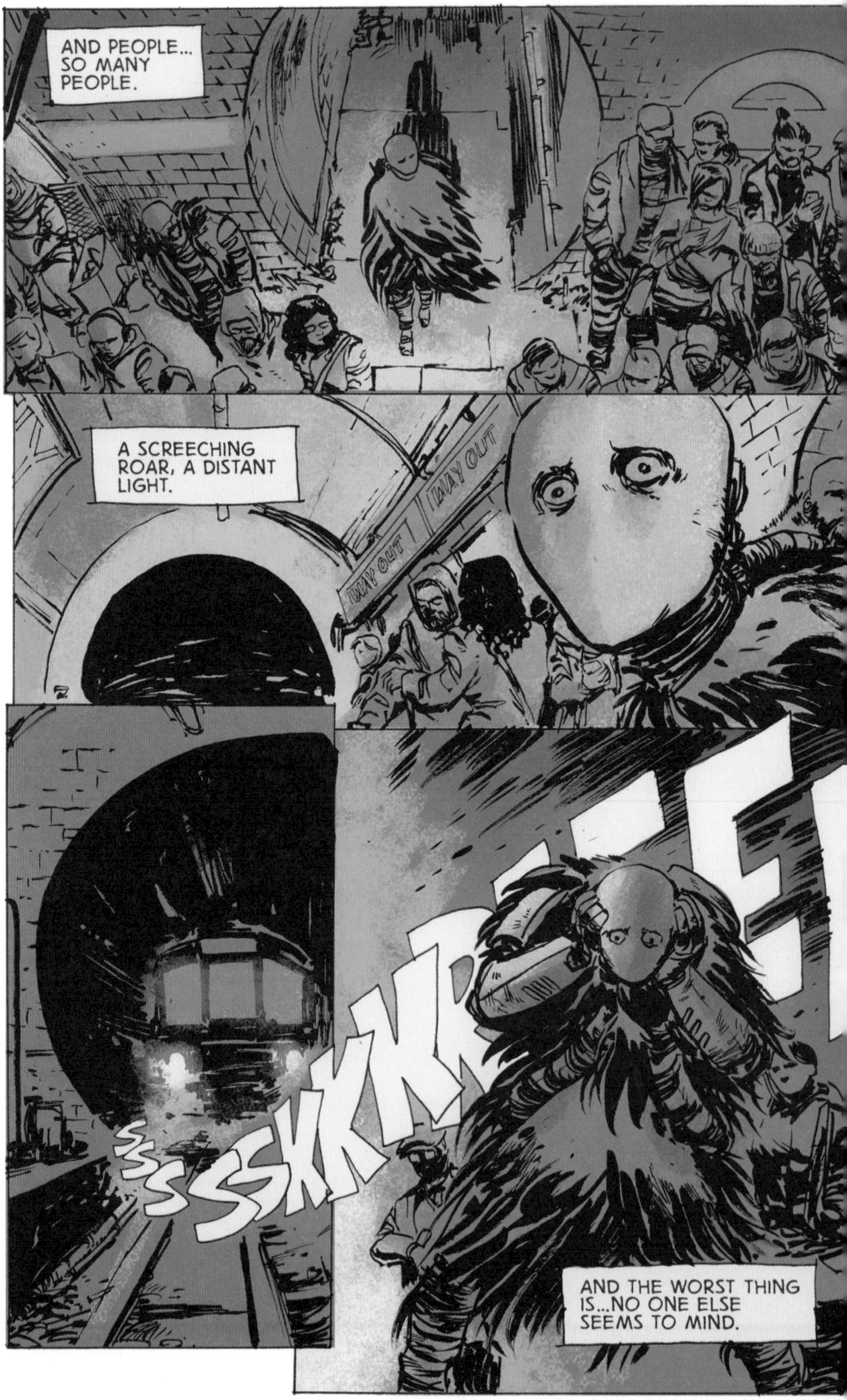
AND PEOPLE... SO MANY PEOPLE.
A SCREECHING ROAR, A DISTANT LIGHT.
WAY OUT
WAY OUT
WAY OUT
SSSSKKR
AND THE WORST THING IS...NO ONE ELSE SEEMS TO MIND.

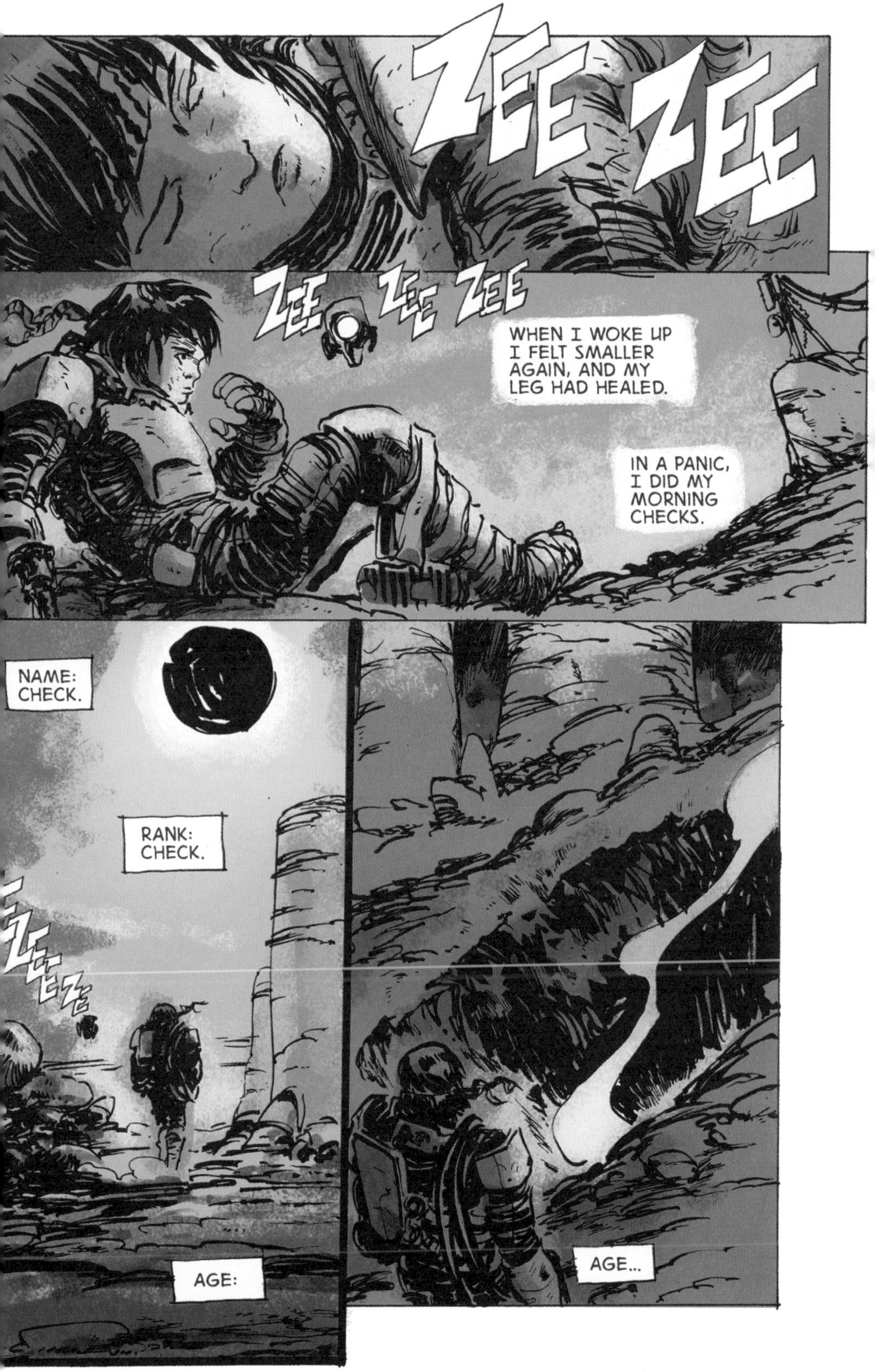
ZEE ZEE
ZEE ZEE ZEE
WHEN I WOKE UP I FELT SMALLER AGAIN, AND MY LEG HAD HEALED.
IN A PANIC, I DID MY MORNING CHECKS.
NAME: CHECK.
RANK: CHECK.
ZEE ZEE ZEE
AGE:
AGE...

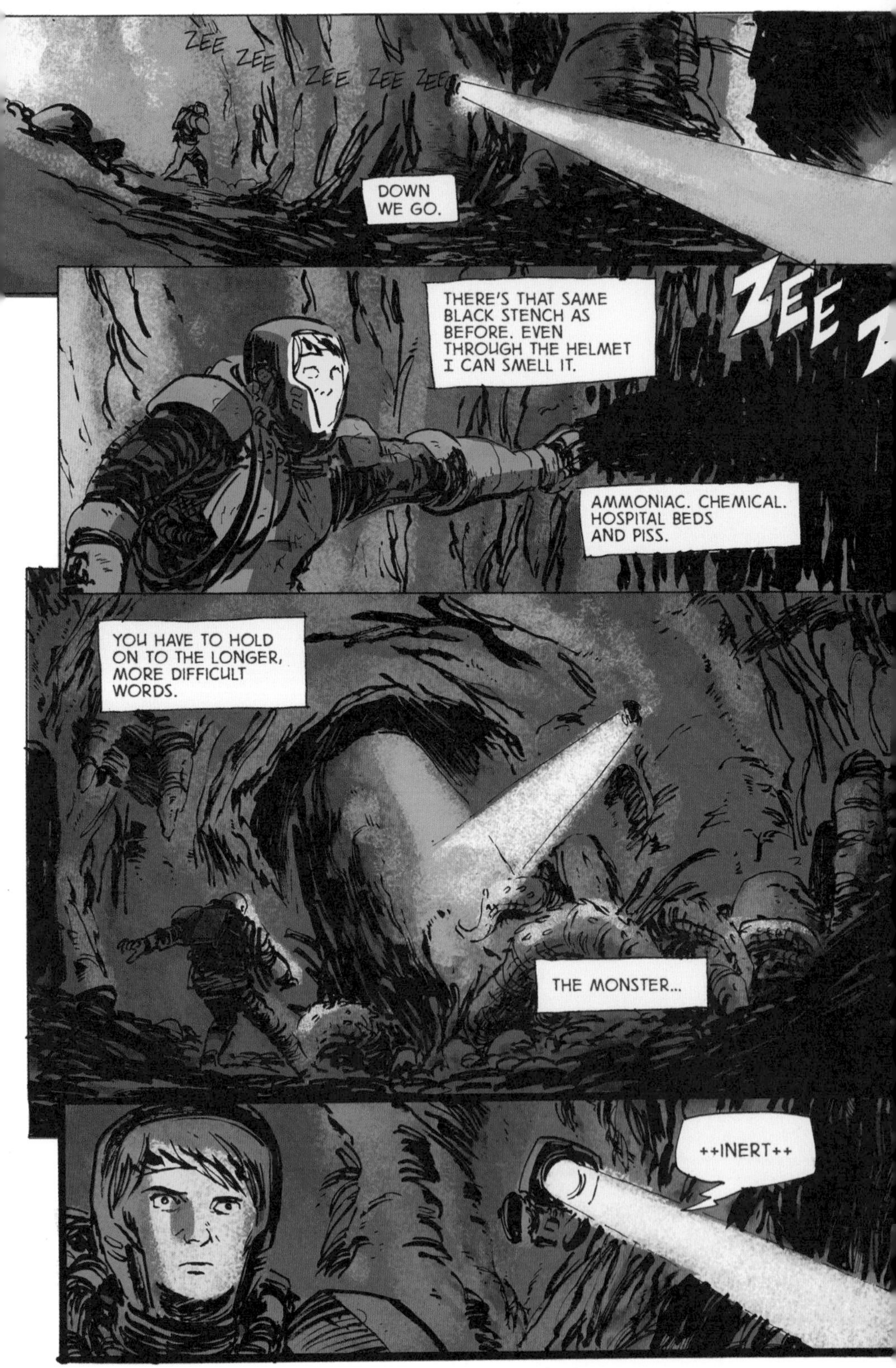
ZEE ZEE ZEE ZEE ZEE
DOWN WE GO.
ZEE Z
THERE'S THAT SAME BLACK STENCH AS BEFORE. EVEN THROUGH THE HELMET I CAN SMELL IT.
AMMONIAC. CHEMICAL. HOSPITAL BEDS AND PISS.
YOU HAVE TO HOLD ON TO THE LONGER, MORE DIFFICULT WORDS.
THE MONSTER...
++INERT++

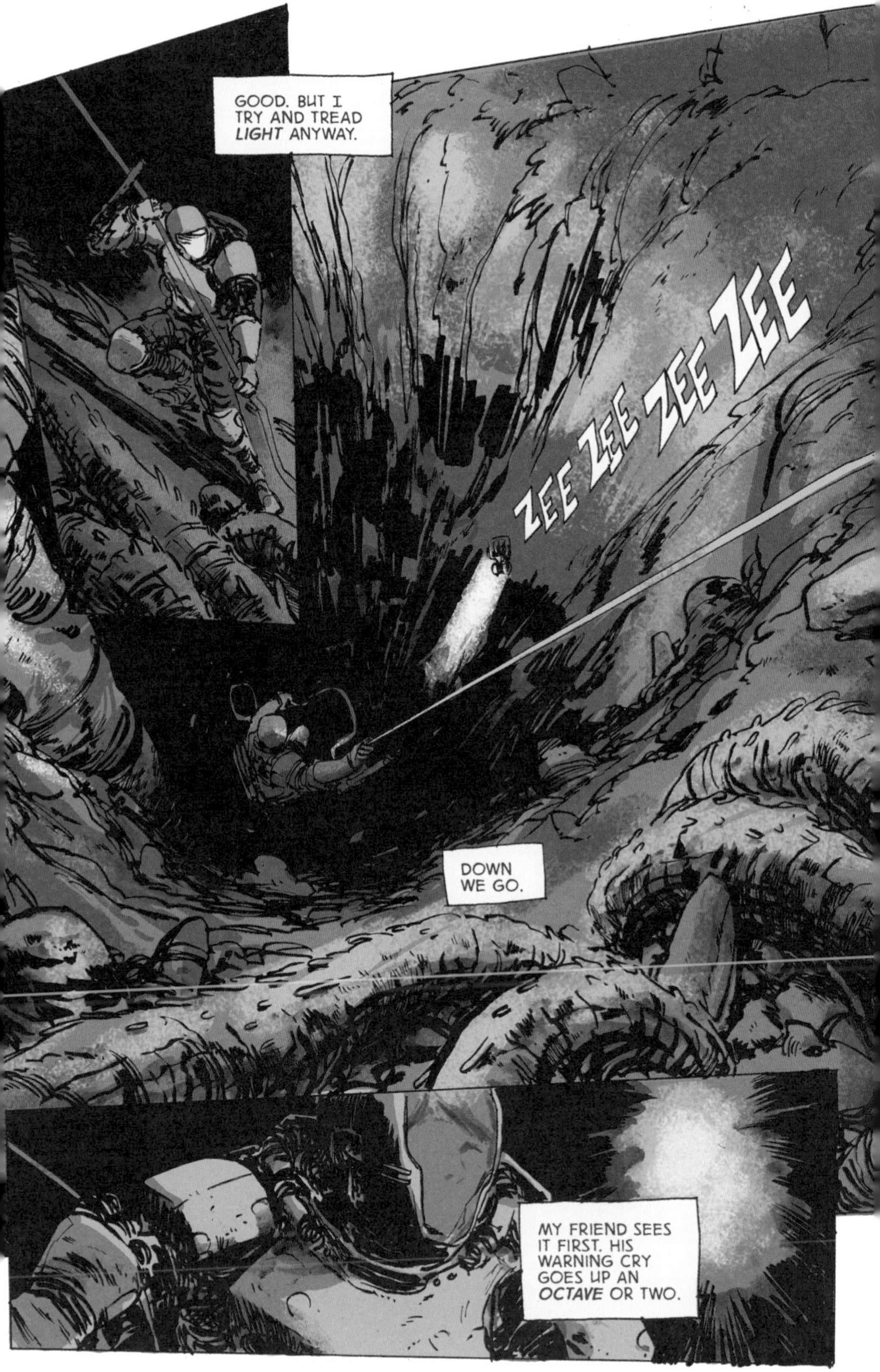
GOOD. BUT I TRY AND TREAD *LIGHT* ANYWAY.
ZEE ZEE ZEE ZEE ZEE
DOWN WE GO.
MY FRIEND SEES IT FIRST. HIS WARNING CRY GOES UP AN *OCTAVE* OR TWO.

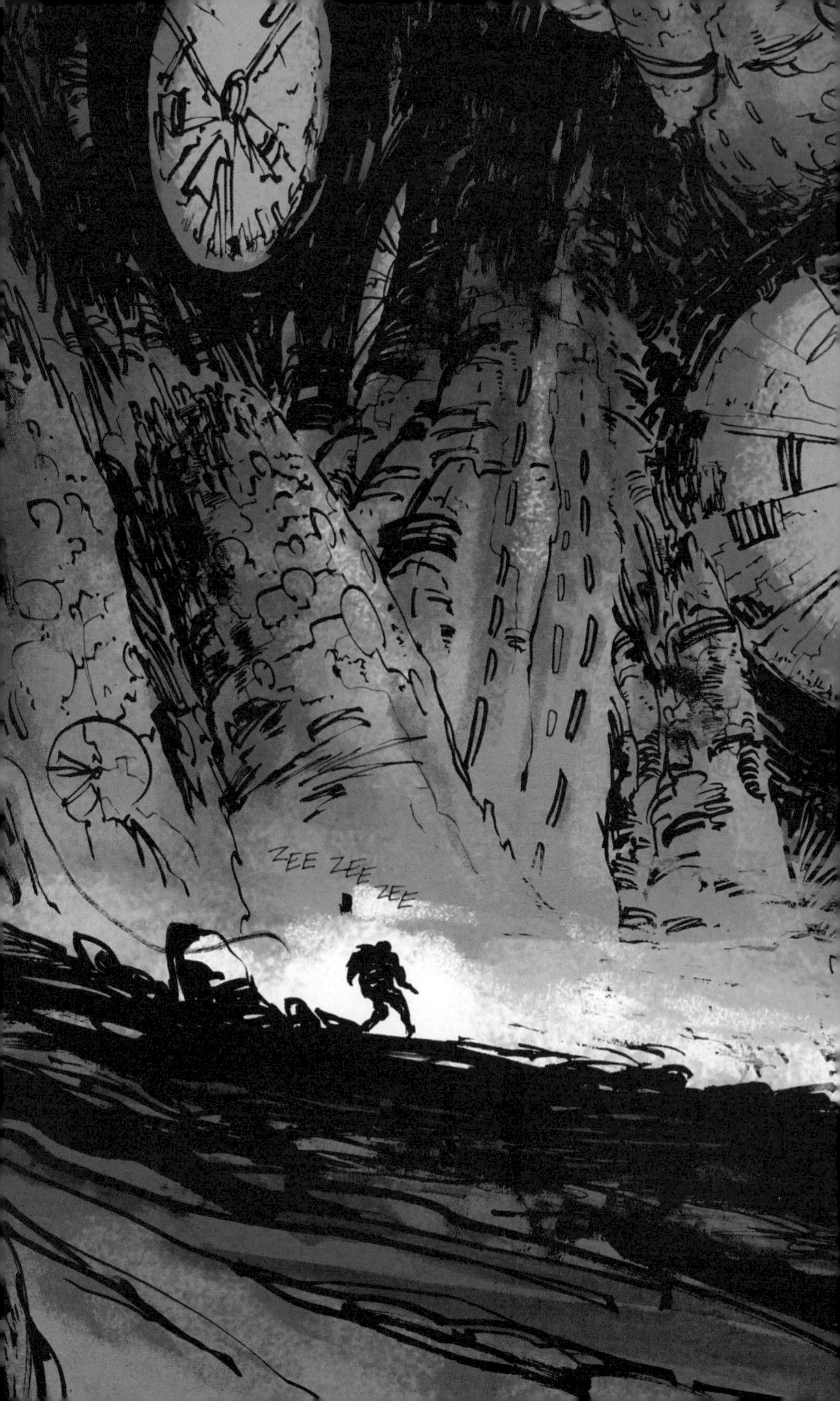
ZEE ZEE ZEE

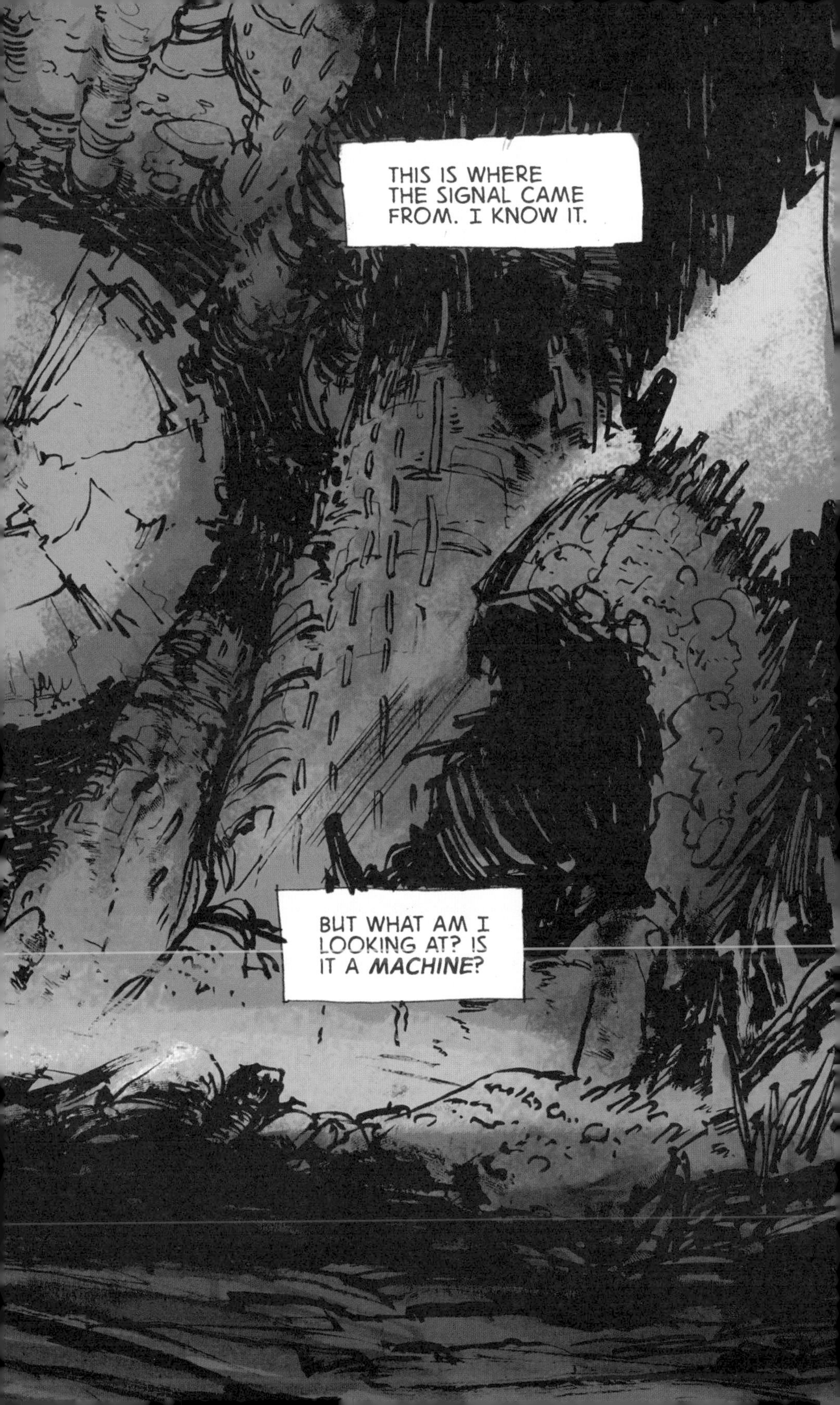
THIS IS WHERE THE SIGNAL CAME FROM. I KNOW IT.
BUT WHAT AM I LOOKING AT? IS IT A *MACHINE*?

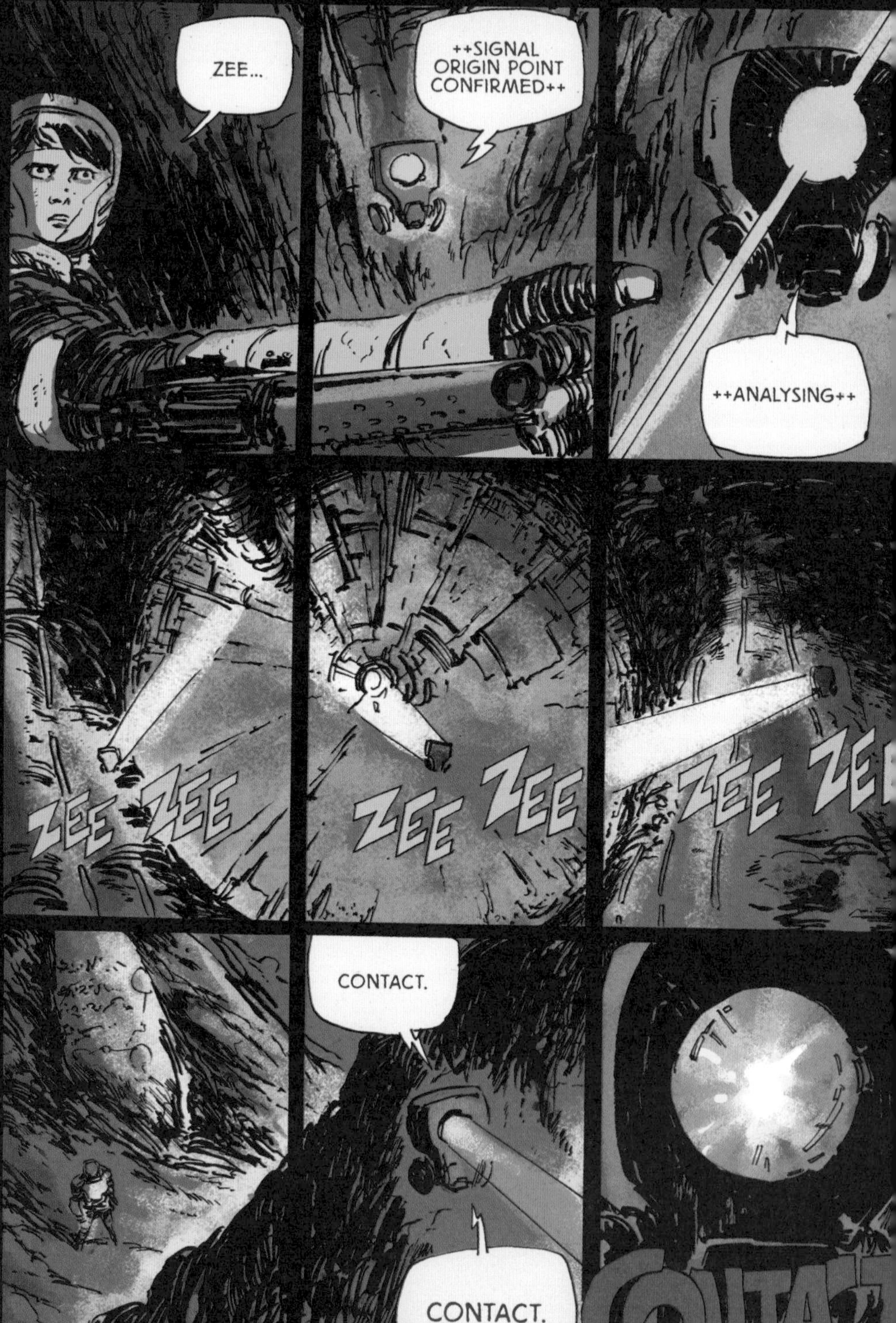
ZEE...
++SIGNAL ORIGIN POINT CONFIRMED++
++ANALYSING++
ZEE ZEE
ZEE ZEE
ZEE ZE
CONTACT.
CONTACT.

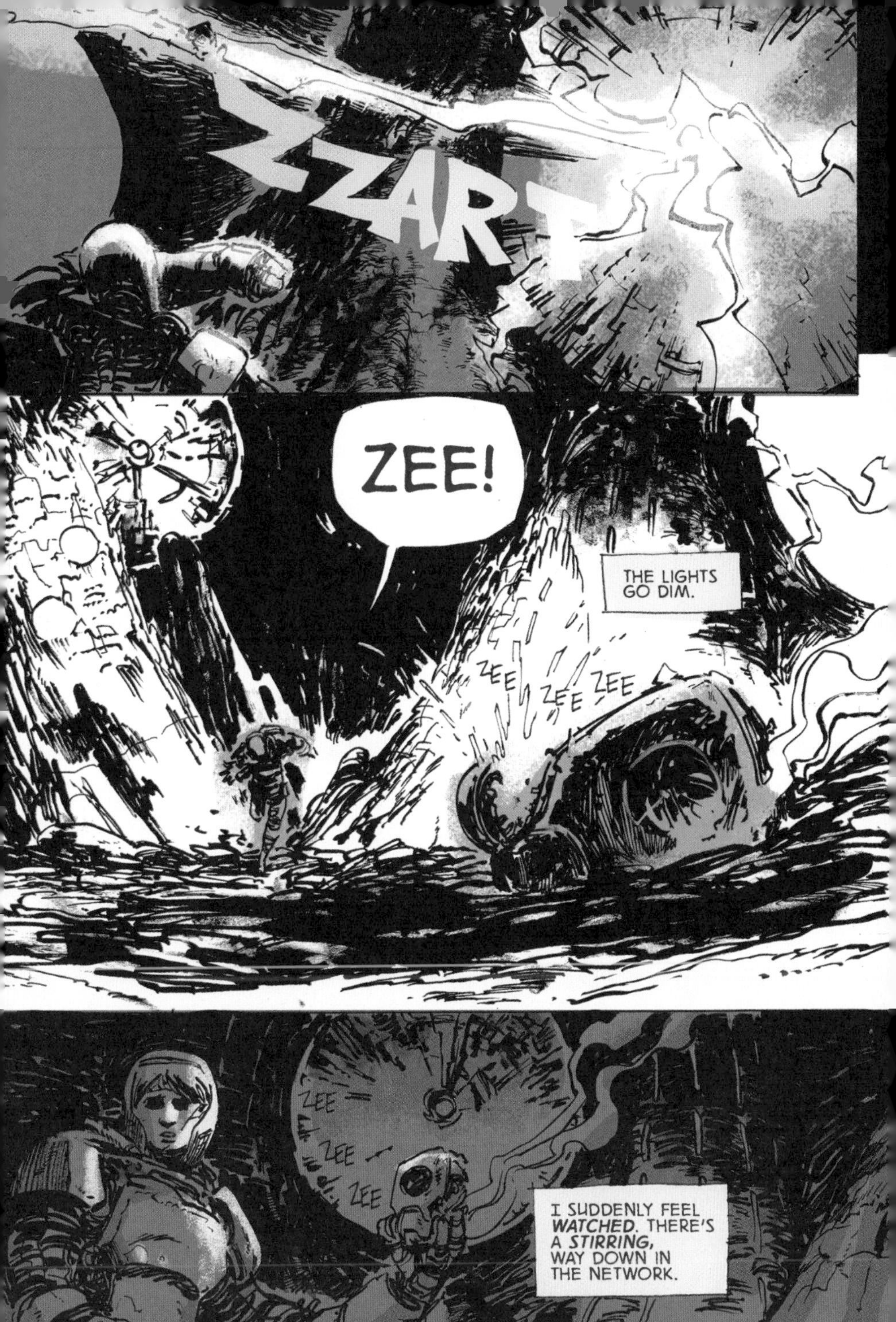
ZZART
ZEE!
THE LIGHTS GO DIM.
ZEE ZEE ZEE
ZEE ZEE ZEE
I SUDDENLY FEEL *WATCHED*. THERE'S A *STIRRING*, WAY DOWN IN THE NETWORK.

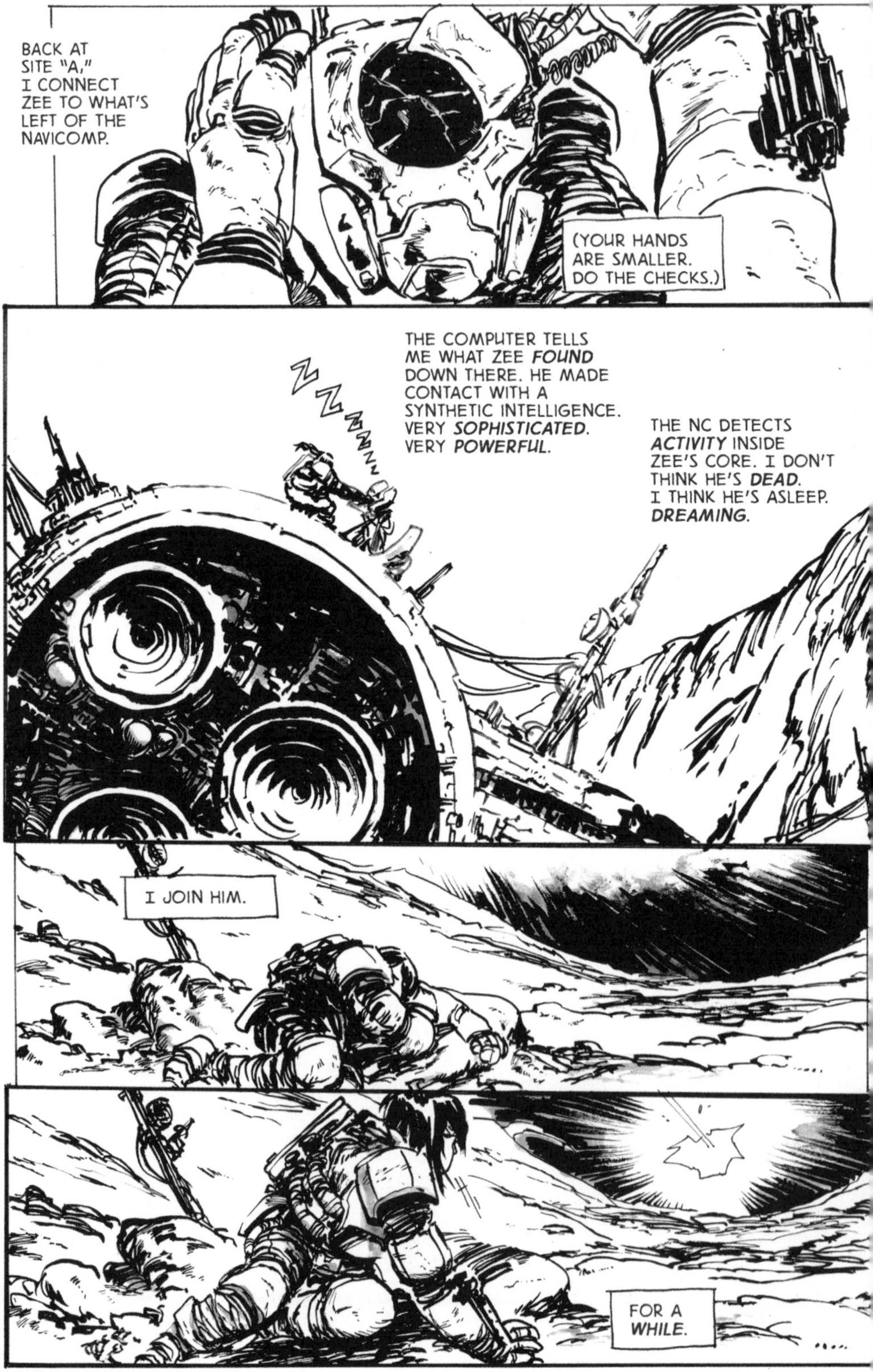
BACK AT SITE "A," I CONNECT ZEE TO WHAT'S LEFT OF THE NAVICOMP.
(YOUR HANDS ARE SMALLER. DO THE CHECKS.)
THE COMPUTER TELLS ME WHAT ZEE FOUND DOWN THERE. HE MADE CONTACT WITH A SYNTHETIC INTELLIGENCE. VERY SOPHISTICATED. VERY POWERFUL.
ZZZZZZZ
THE NC DETECTS ACTIVITY INSIDE ZEE'S CORE. I DON'T THINK HE'S DEAD. I THINK HE'S ASLEEP. DREAMING.
I JOIN HIM.
FOR A WHILE.

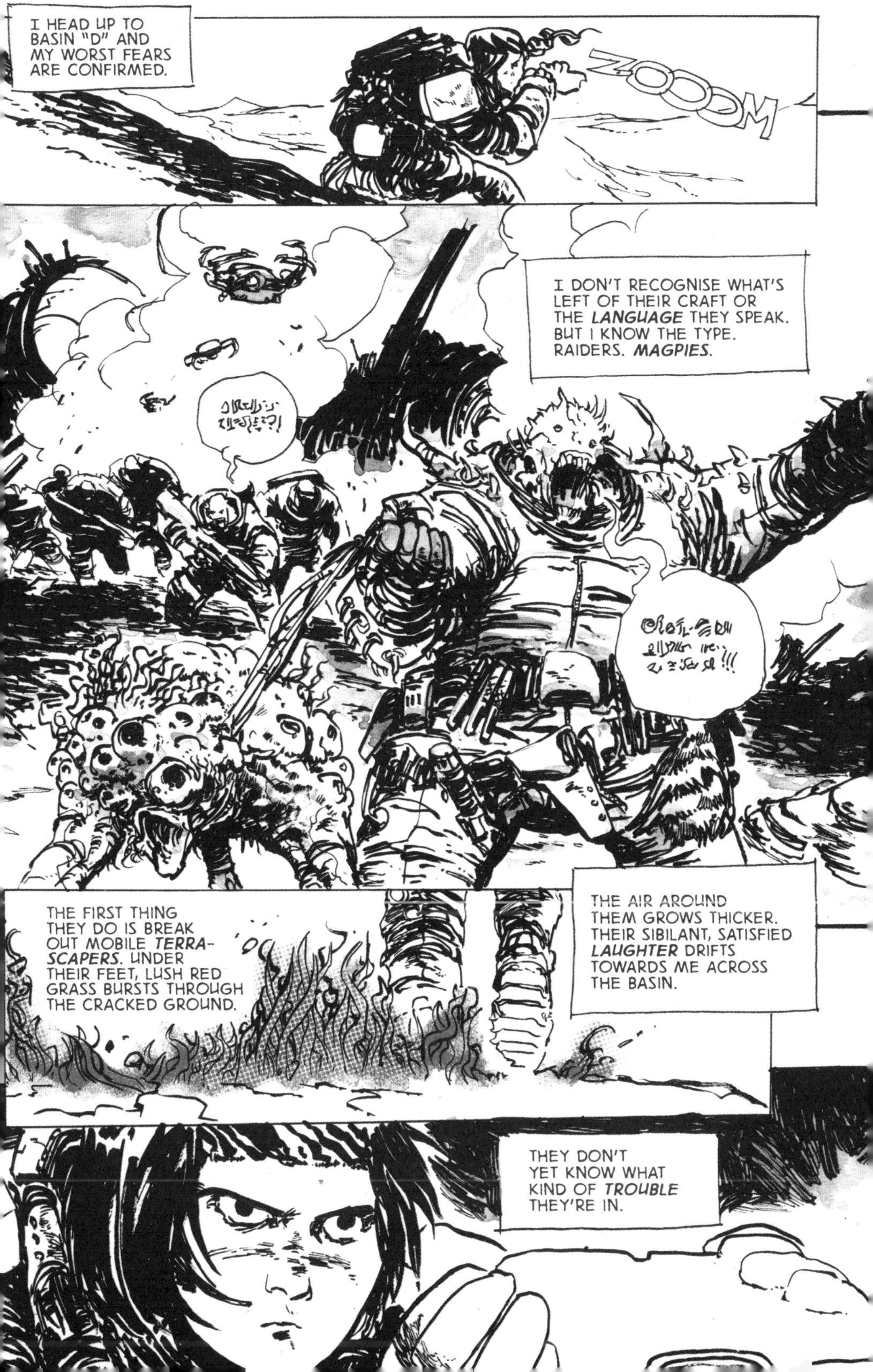
I HEAD UP TO BASIN "D" AND MY WORST FEARS ARE CONFIRMED.
ZOOOM
I DON'T RECOGNISE WHAT'S LEFT OF THEIR CRAFT OR THE *LANGUAGE* THEY SPEAK. BUT I KNOW THE TYPE. RAIDERS. *MAGPIES*.
THE FIRST THING THEY DO IS BREAK OUT MOBILE *TERRA-SCAPERS*. UNDER THEIR FEET, LUSH RED GRASS BURSTS THROUGH THE CRACKED GROUND.
THE AIR AROUND THEM GROWS THICKER. THEIR SIBILANT, SATISFIED *LAUGHTER* DRIFTS TOWARDS ME ACROSS THE BASIN.
THEY DON'T YET KNOW WHAT KIND OF *TROUBLE* THEY'RE IN.

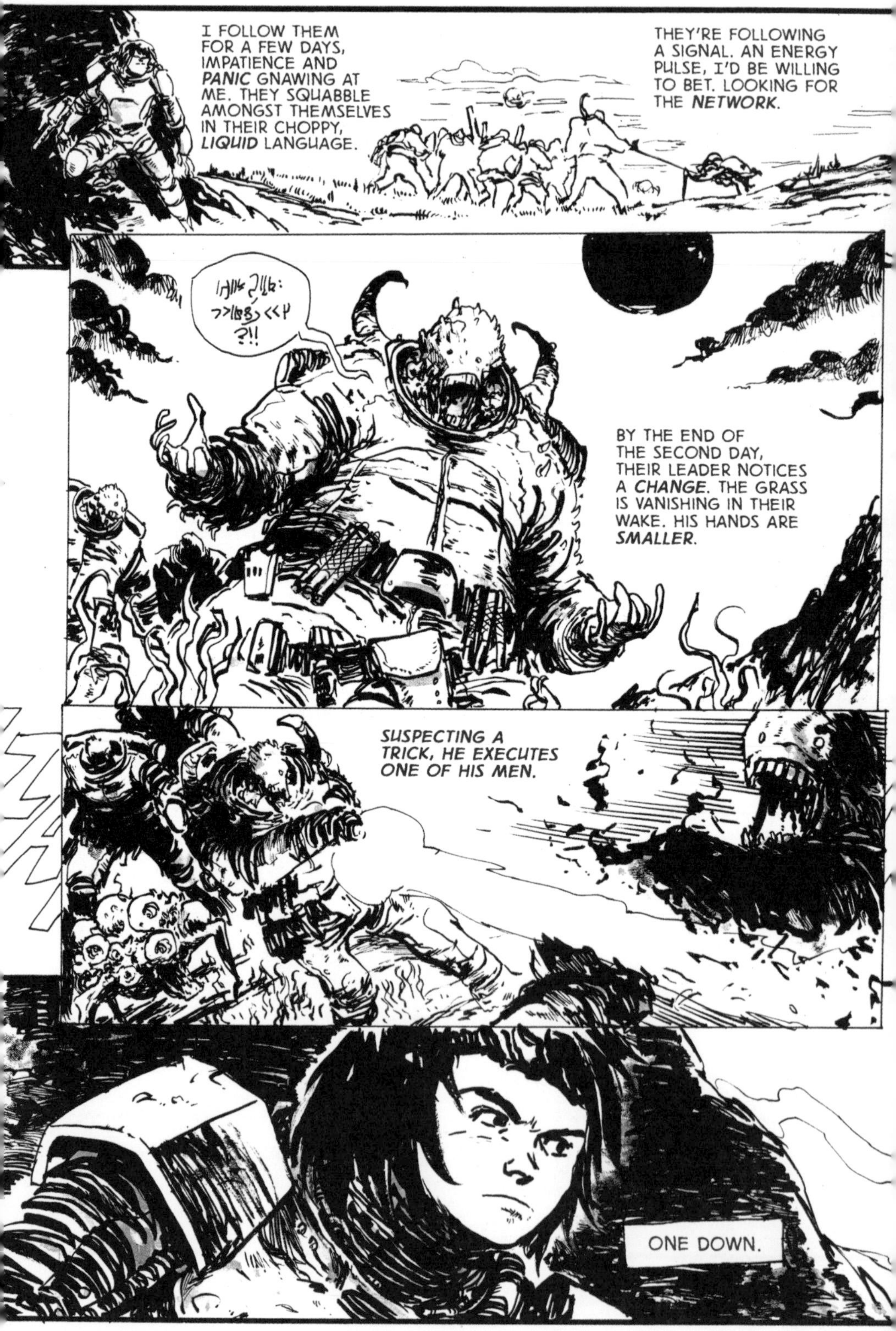
I FOLLOW THEM FOR A FEW DAYS, IMPATIENCE AND *PANIC* GNAWING AT ME. THEY SQUABBLE AMONGST THEMSELVES IN THEIR CHOPPY, *LIQUID* LANGUAGE.
THEY'RE FOLLOWING A SIGNAL. AN ENERGY PULSE, I'D BE WILLING TO BET. LOOKING FOR THE *NETWORK*.
BY THE END OF THE SECOND DAY, THEIR LEADER NOTICES A *CHANGE*. THE GRASS IS VANISHING IN THEIR WAKE. HIS HANDS ARE *SMALLER*.
SUSPECTING A TRICK, HE EXECUTES ONE OF HIS MEN.
ONE DOWN.

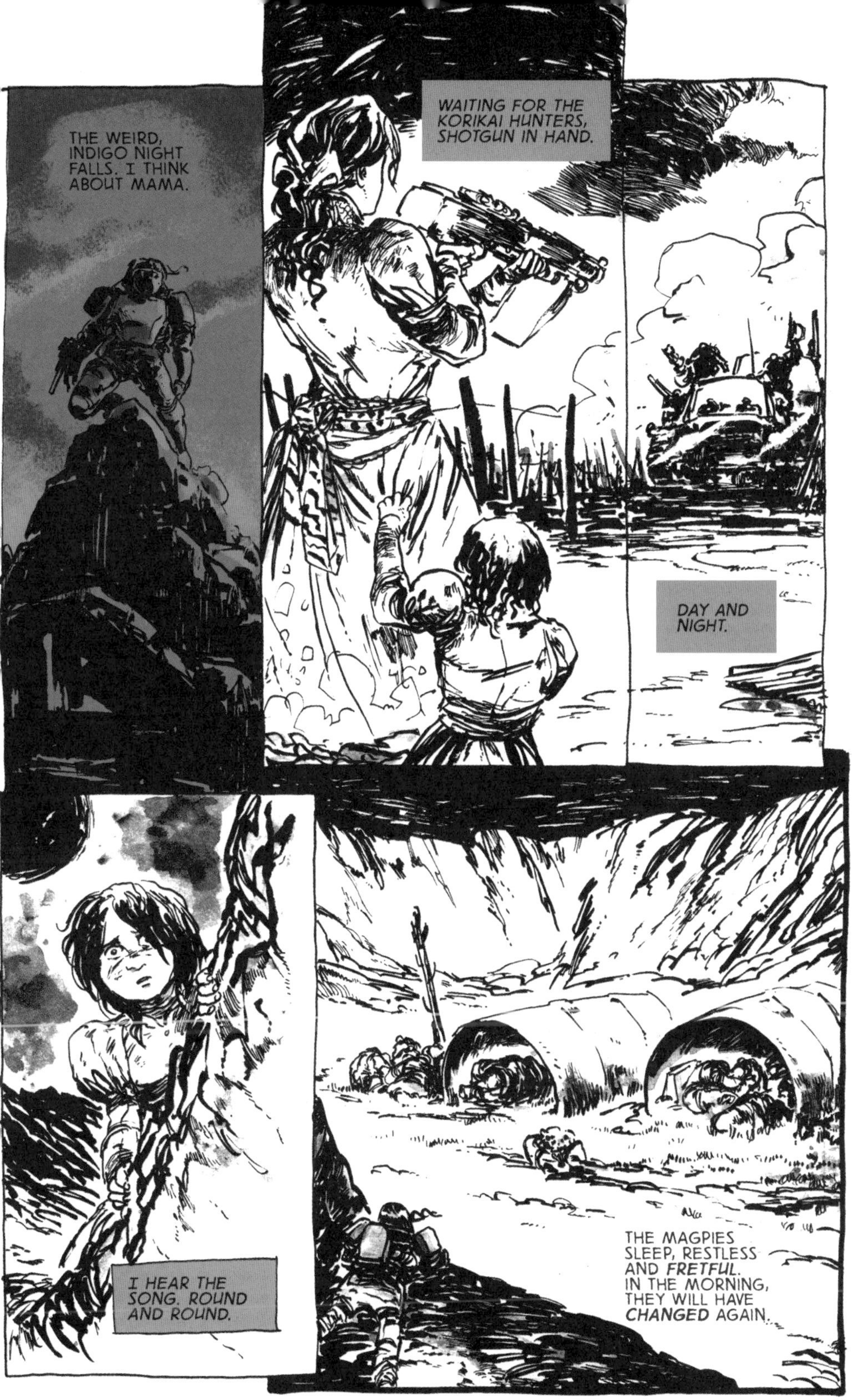
THE WEIRD, INDIGO NIGHT FALLS. I THINK ABOUT MAMA.
WAITING FOR THE KORIKAI HUNTERS, SHOTGUN IN HAND.
DAY AND NIGHT.
I HEAR THE SONG. ROUND AND ROUND.
THE MAGPIES SLEEP, RESTLESS AND FRETFUL. IN THE MORNING, THEY WILL HAVE CHANGED AGAIN.

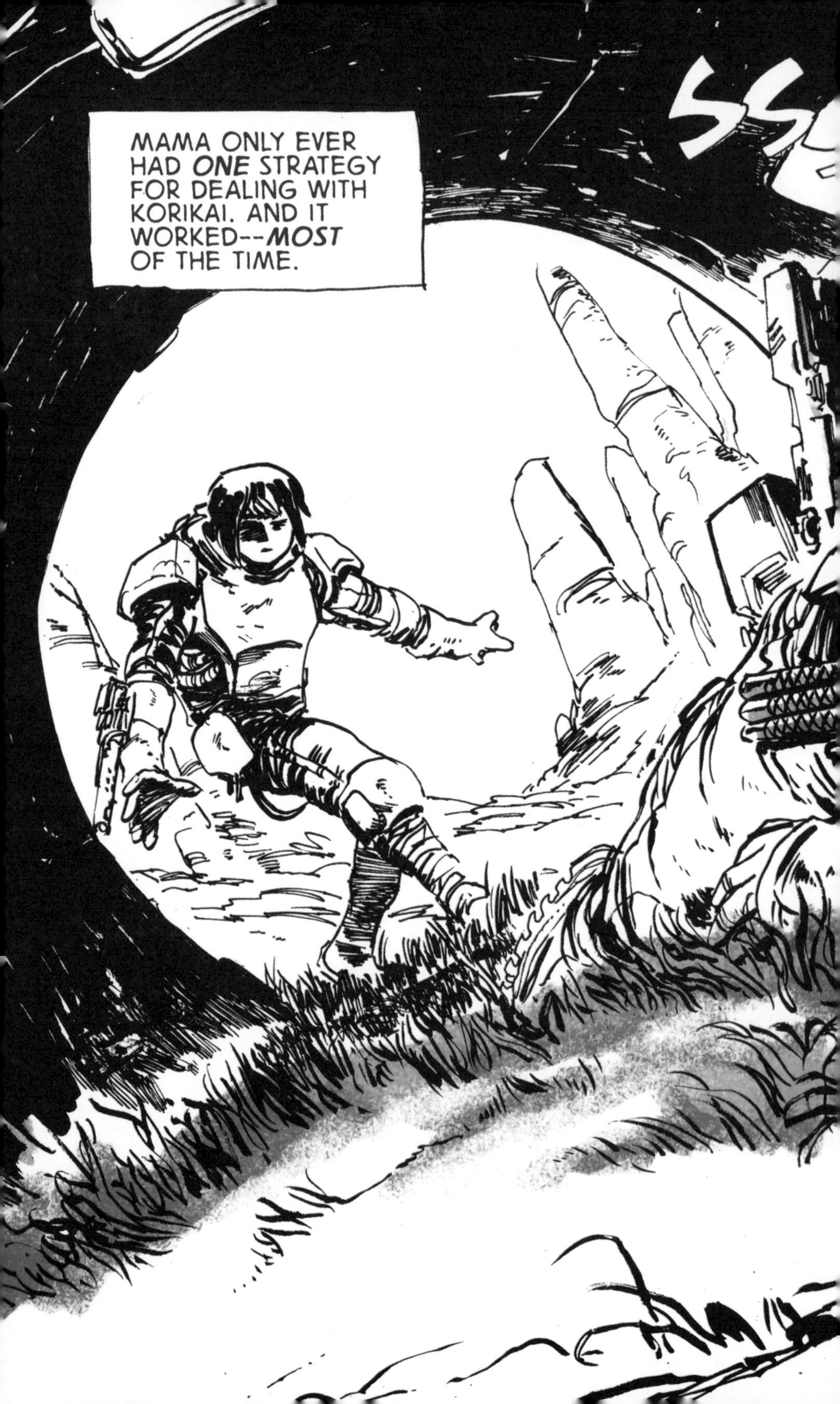
MAMA ONLY EVER HAD *ONE* STRATEGY FOR DEALING WITH KORIKAI. AND IT WORKED--*MOST* OF THE TIME.

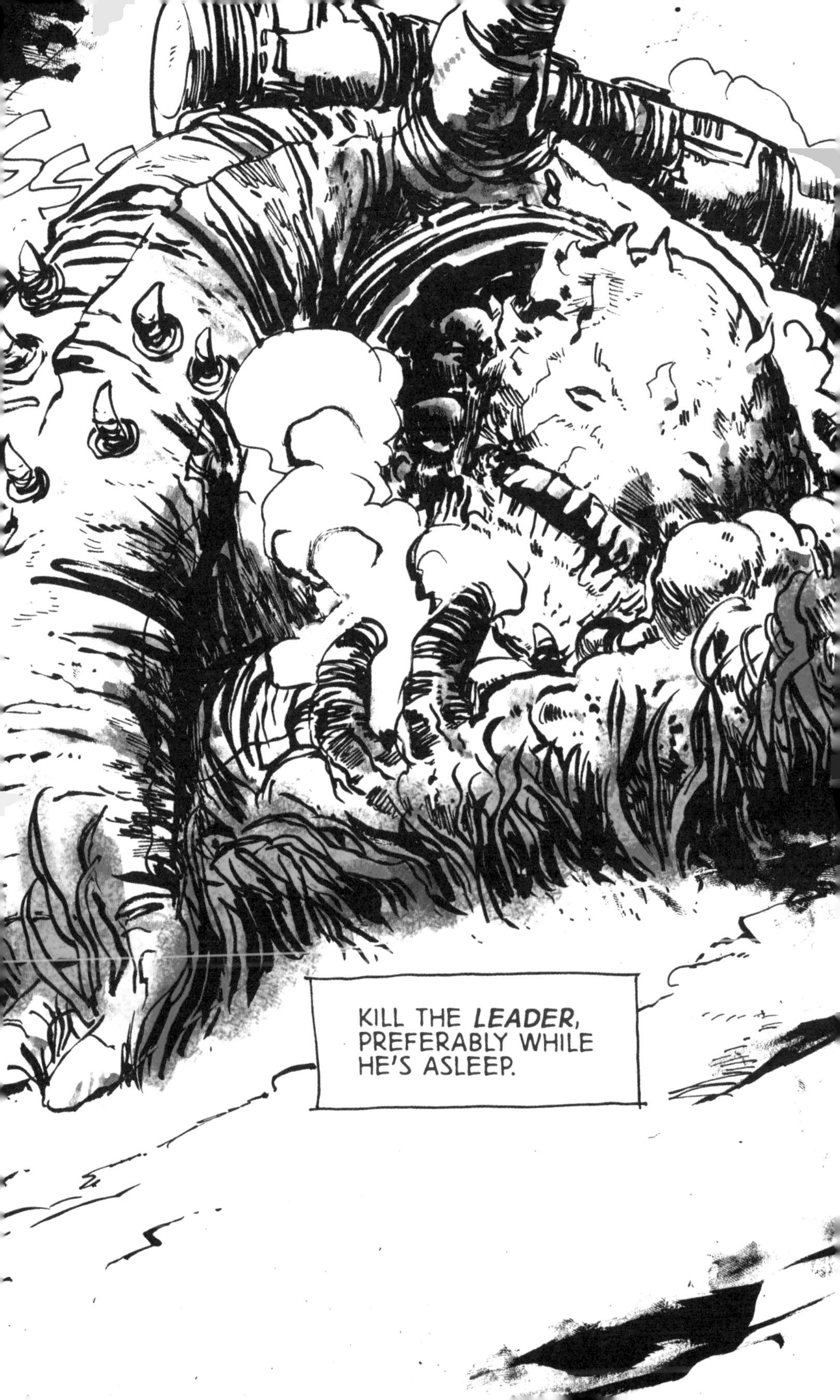
KILL THE *LEADER*, PREFERABLY WHILE HE'S ASLEEP.

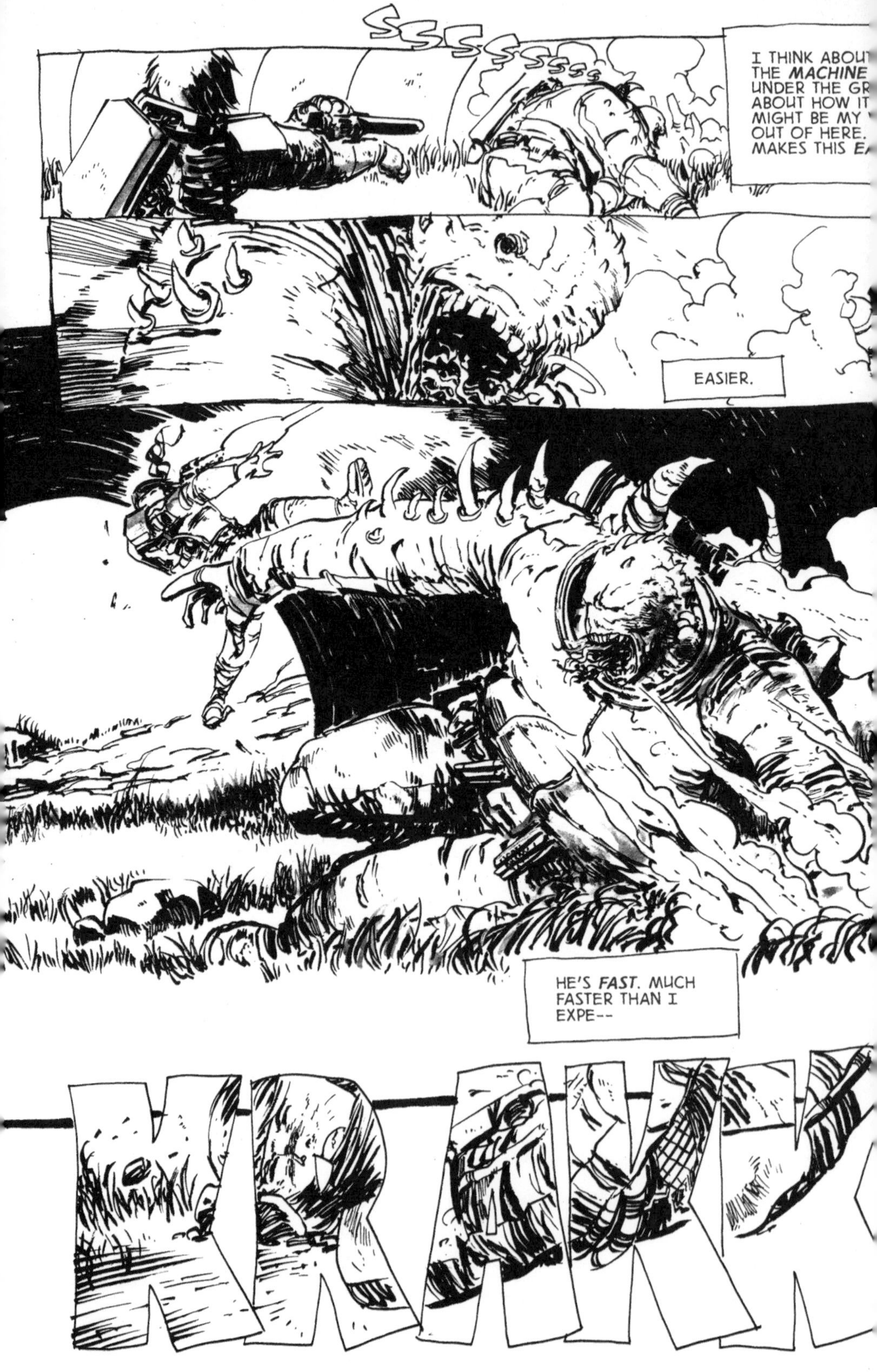

SSSSSSSSsss
I THINK ABOUT THE MACHINE UNDER THE GR ABOUT HOW IT MIGHT BE MY OUT OF HERE. MAKES THIS E
EASIER.
HE'S FAST. MUCH FASTER THAN I EXPE--
KRAKK

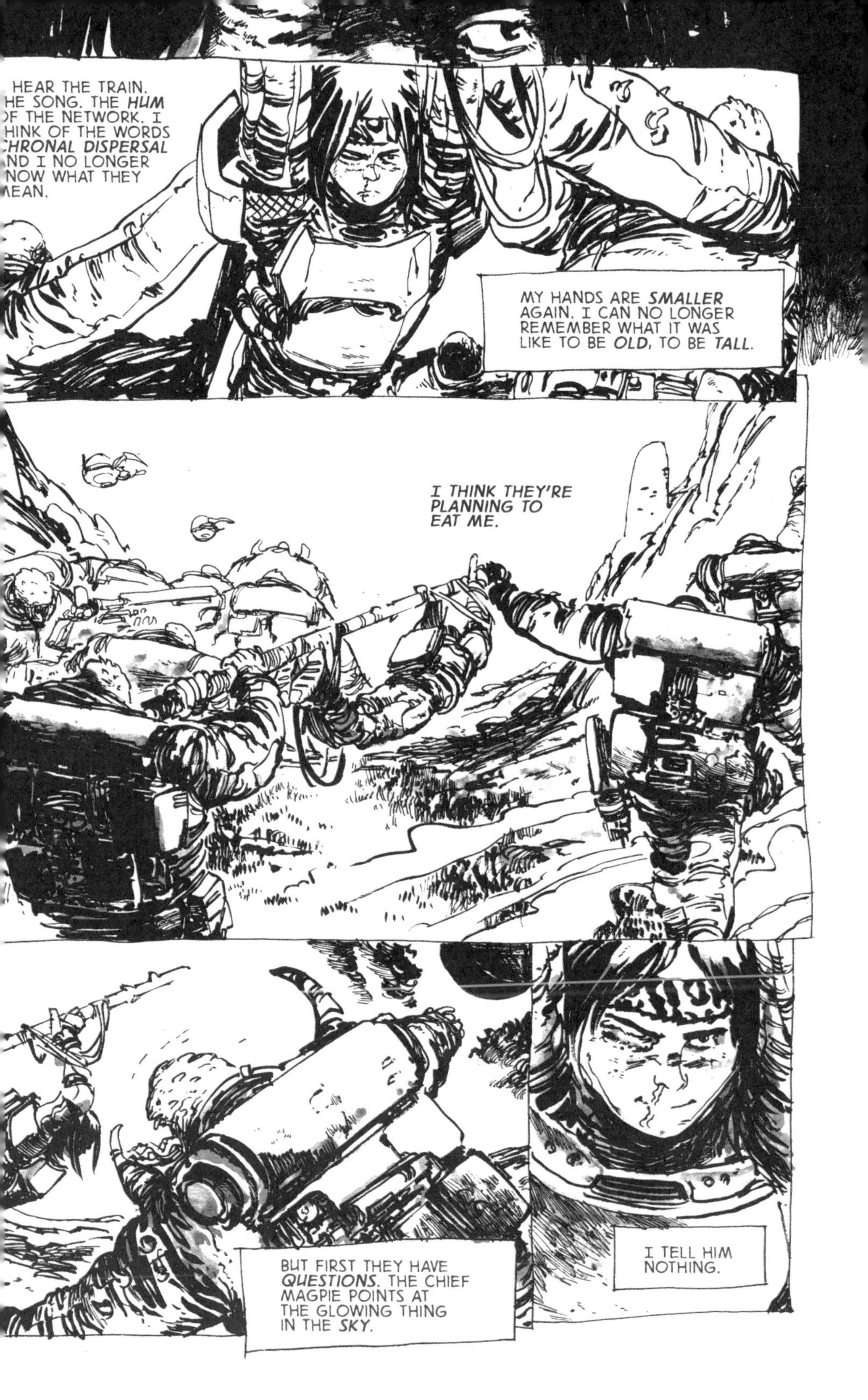
HEAR THE TRAIN. HE SONG. THE *HUM* OF THE NETWORK. I HINK OF THE WORDS *CHRONAL DISPERSAL* ND I NO LONGER NOW WHAT THEY MEAN.
MY HANDS ARE *SMALLER* AGAIN. I CAN NO LONGER REMEMBER WHAT IT WAS LIKE TO BE *OLD*, TO BE *TALL*.
I THINK THEY'RE PLANNING TO EAT ME.
BUT FIRST THEY HAVE *QUESTIONS*. THE CHIEF MAGPIE POINTS AT THE GLOWING THING IN THE *SKY*.
I TELL HIM NOTHING.

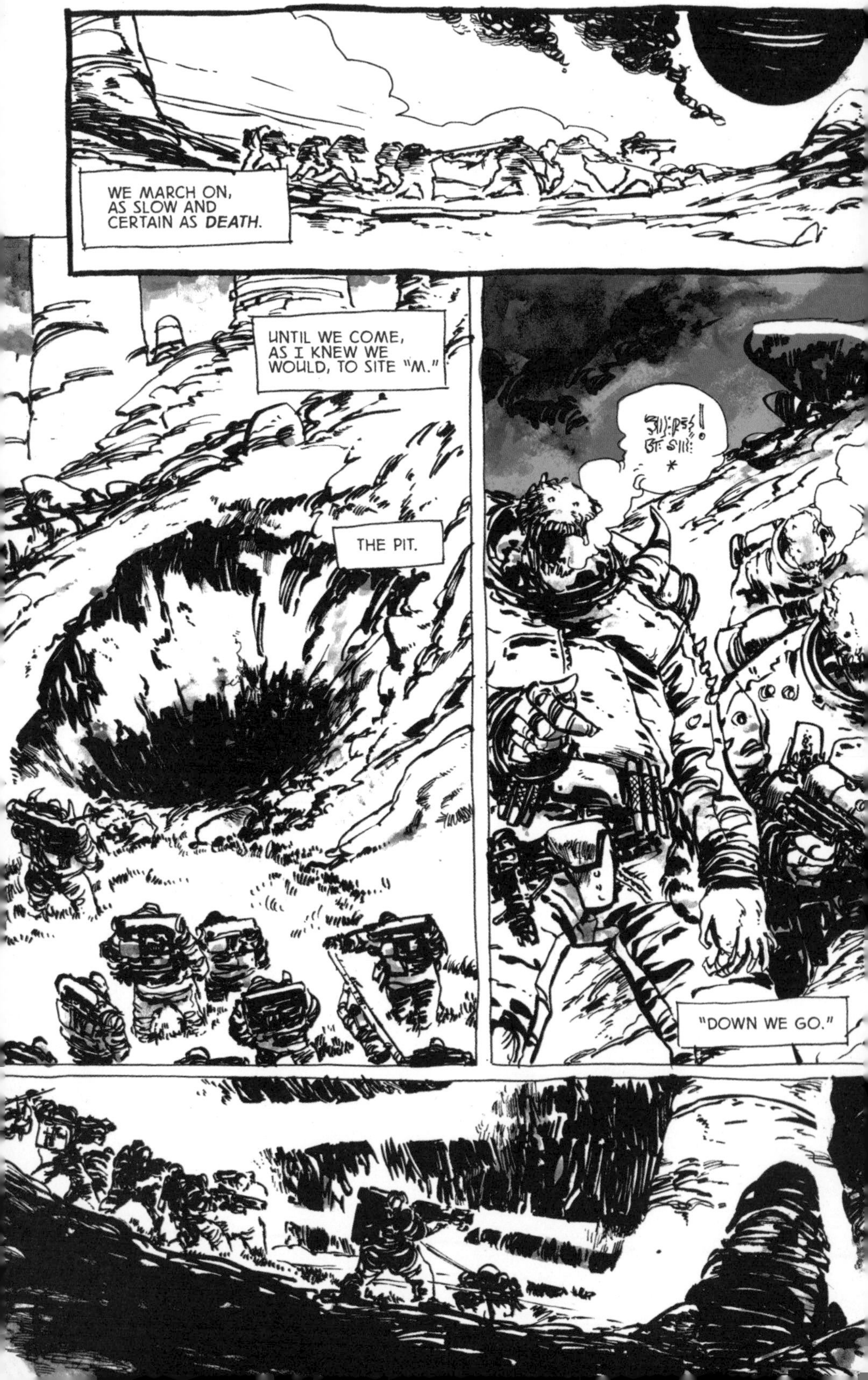
WE MARCH ON, AS SLOW AND CERTAIN AS *DEATH*.
UNTIL WE COME, AS I KNEW WE WOULD, TO SITE "M."
THE PIT.
"DOWN WE GO."

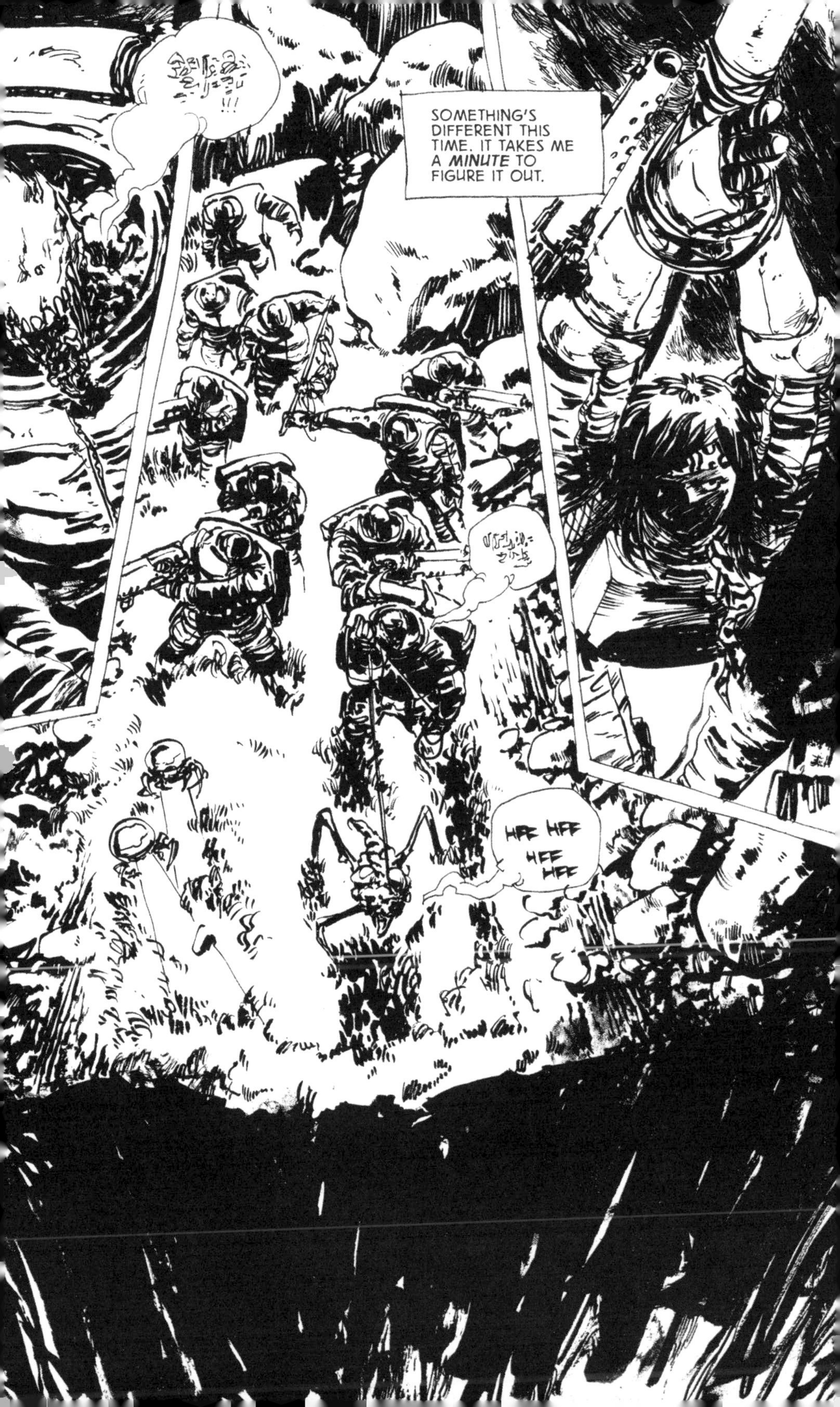

SOMETHING'S DIFFERENT THIS TIME. IT TAKES ME A *MINUTE* TO FIGURE IT OUT.
HFF HFF HFF HFF

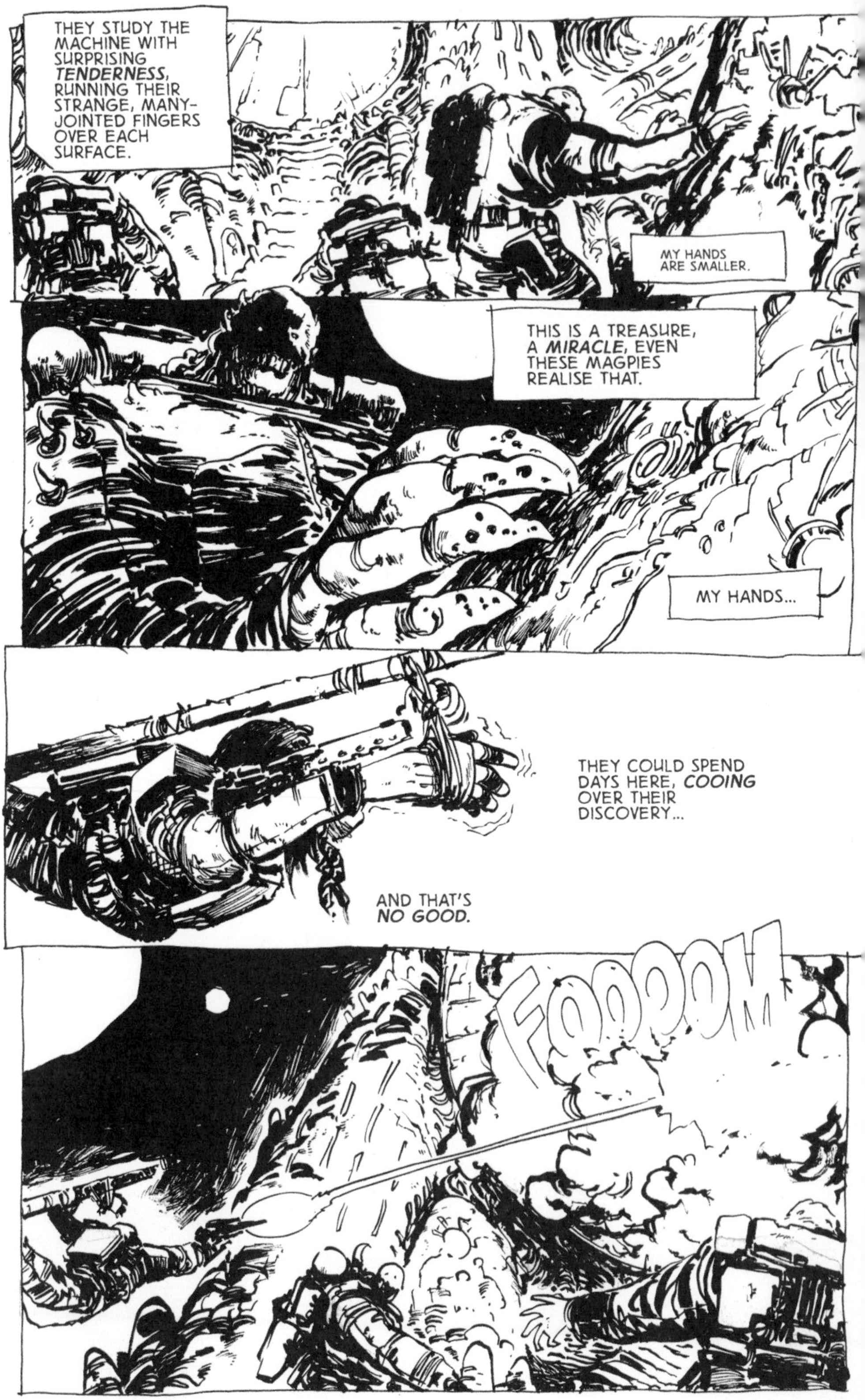
THEY STUDY THE MACHINE WITH SURPRISING **TENDERNESS**, RUNNING THEIR STRANGE, MANY-JOINTED FINGERS OVER EACH SURFACE.
MY HANDS ARE SMALLER.
THIS IS A TREASURE, A **MIRACLE**, EVEN THESE MAGPIES REALISE THAT.
MY HANDS...
THEY COULD SPEND DAYS HERE, **COOING** OVER THEIR DISCOVERY...
AND THAT'S **NO GOOD.**
FOOOOM

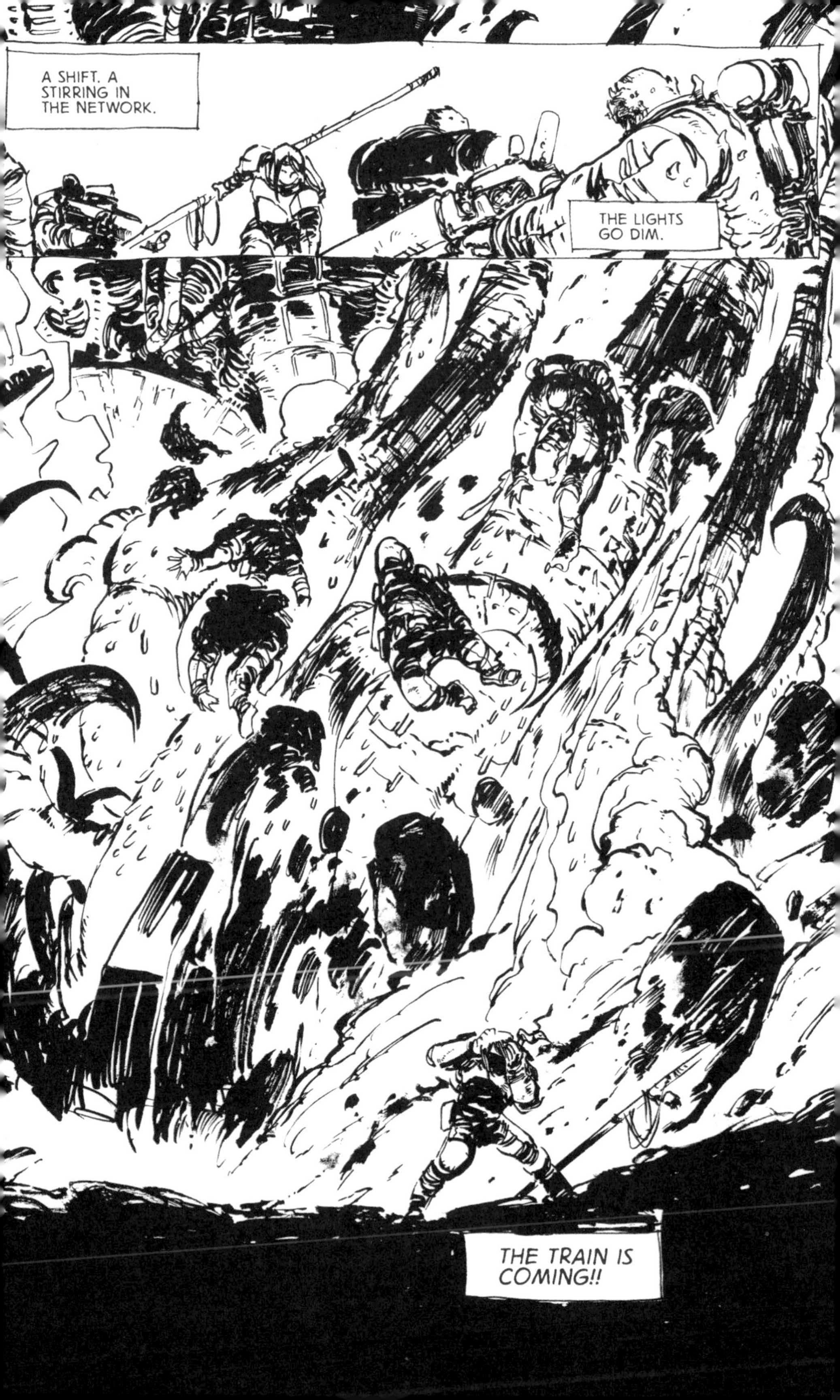
A SHIFT. A STIRRING IN THE NETWORK.
THE LIGHTS GO DIM.
THE TRAIN IS COMING!!

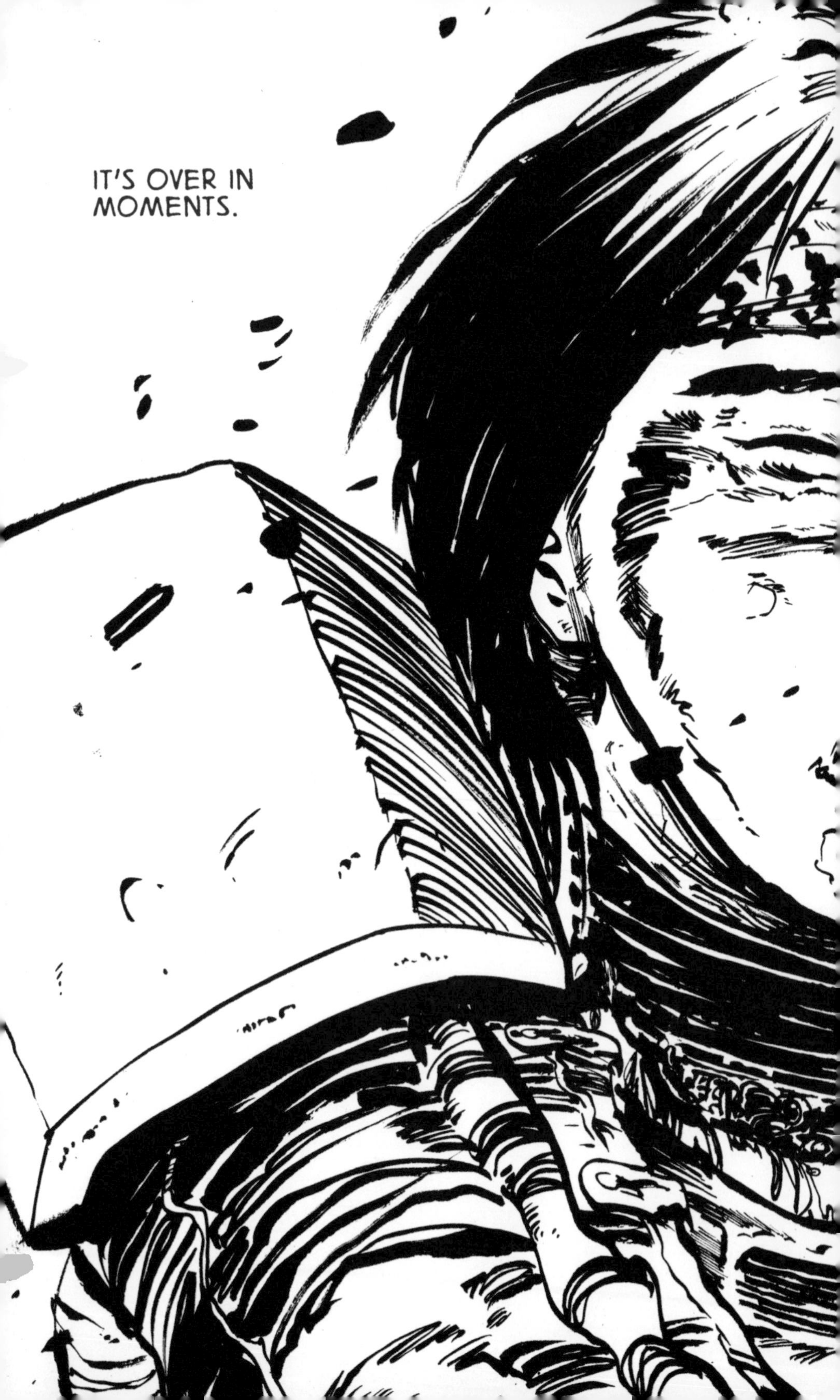
IT'S OVER IN MOMENTS.

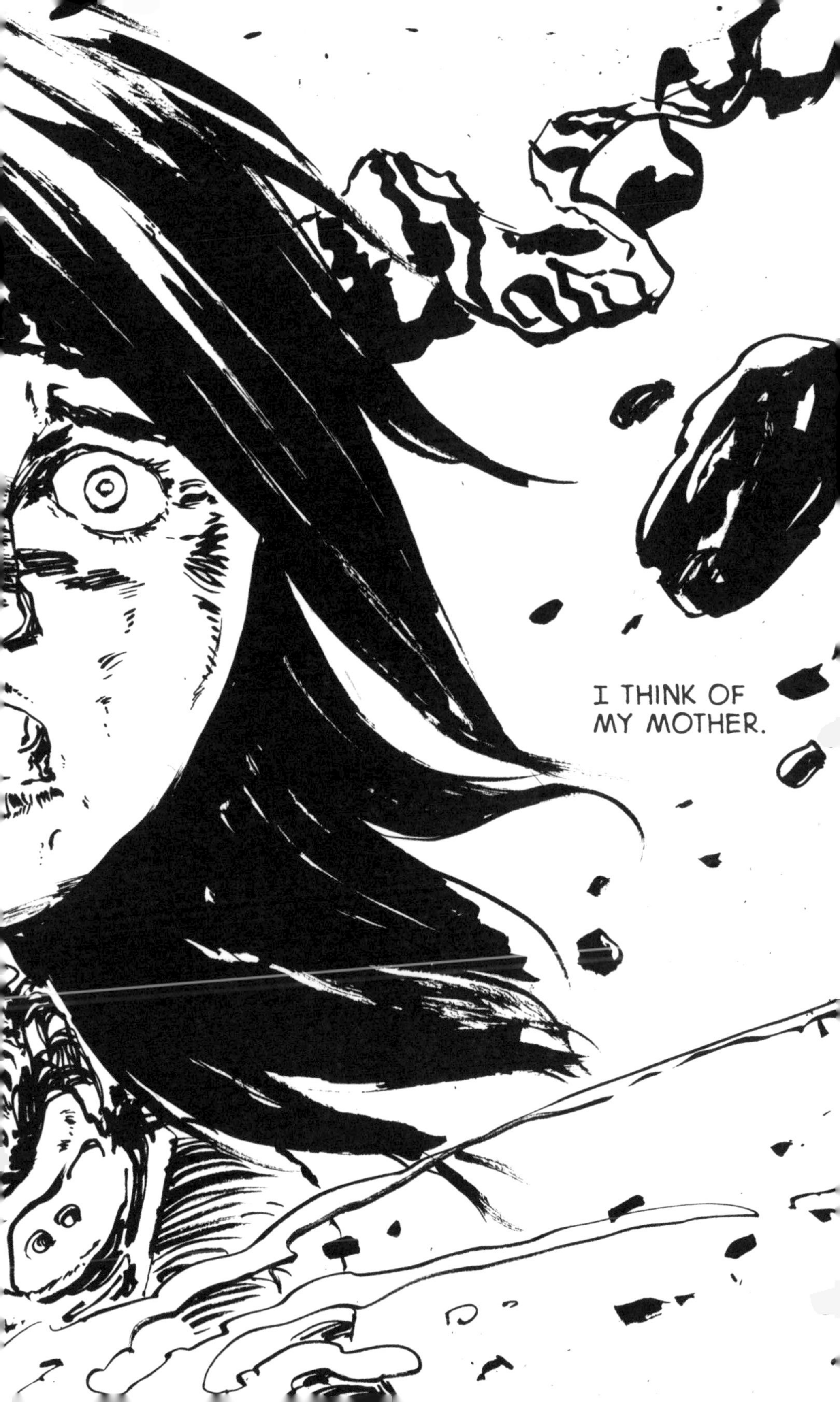
I THINK OF MY MOTHER.

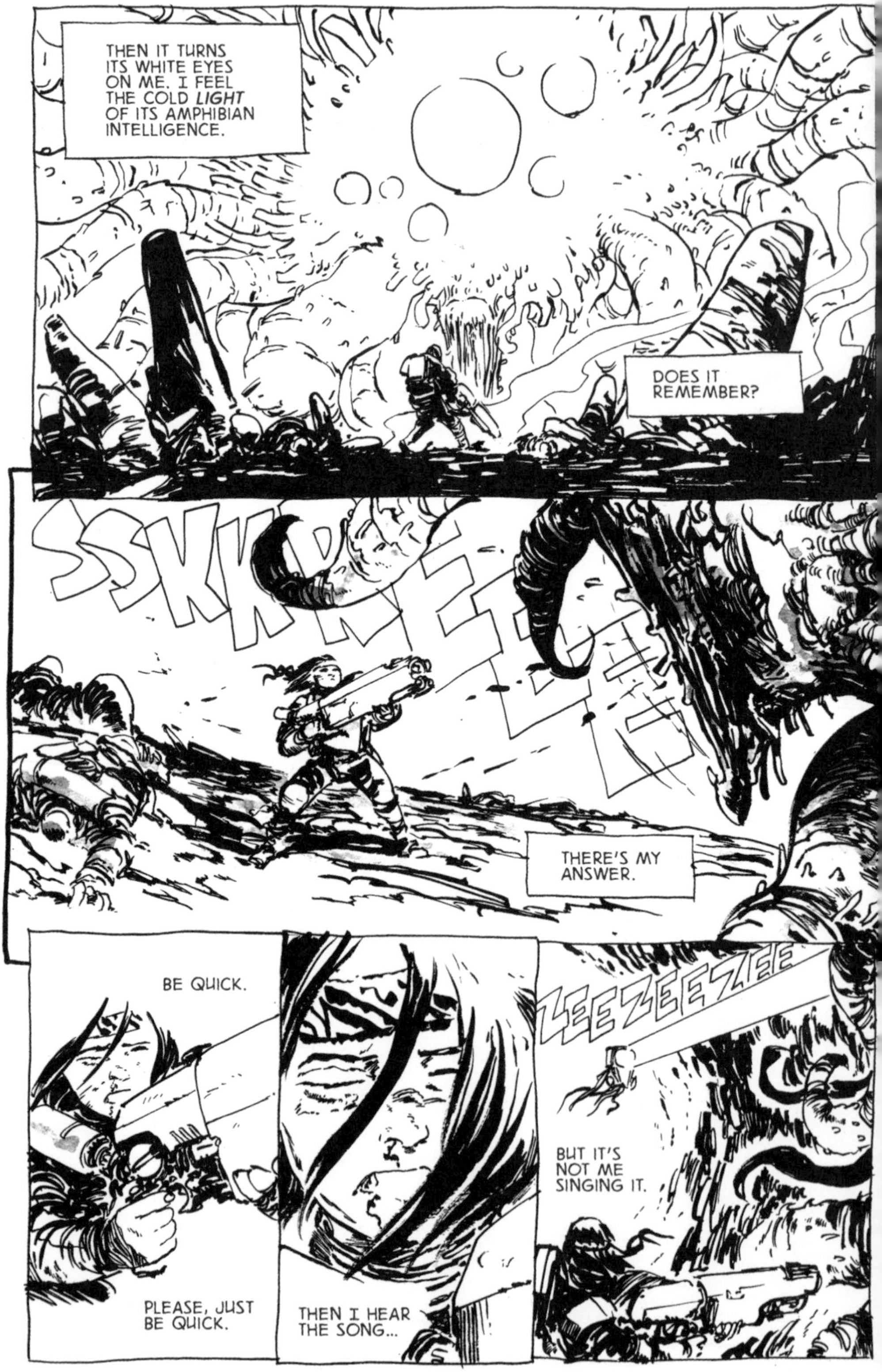
THEN IT TURNS ITS WHITE EYES ON ME. I FEEL THE COLD *LIGHT* OF ITS AMPHIBIAN INTELLIGENCE.
DOES IT REMEMBER?
SSKKREEE
THERE'S MY ANSWER.
BE QUICK.
PLEASE, JUST BE QUICK.
THEN I HEAR THE SONG...
ZEEZEEEZEE
BUT IT'S NOT ME SINGING IT.

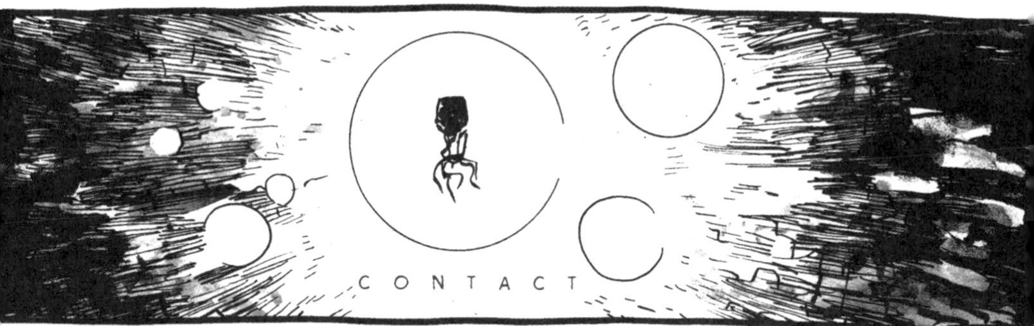
CONTACT

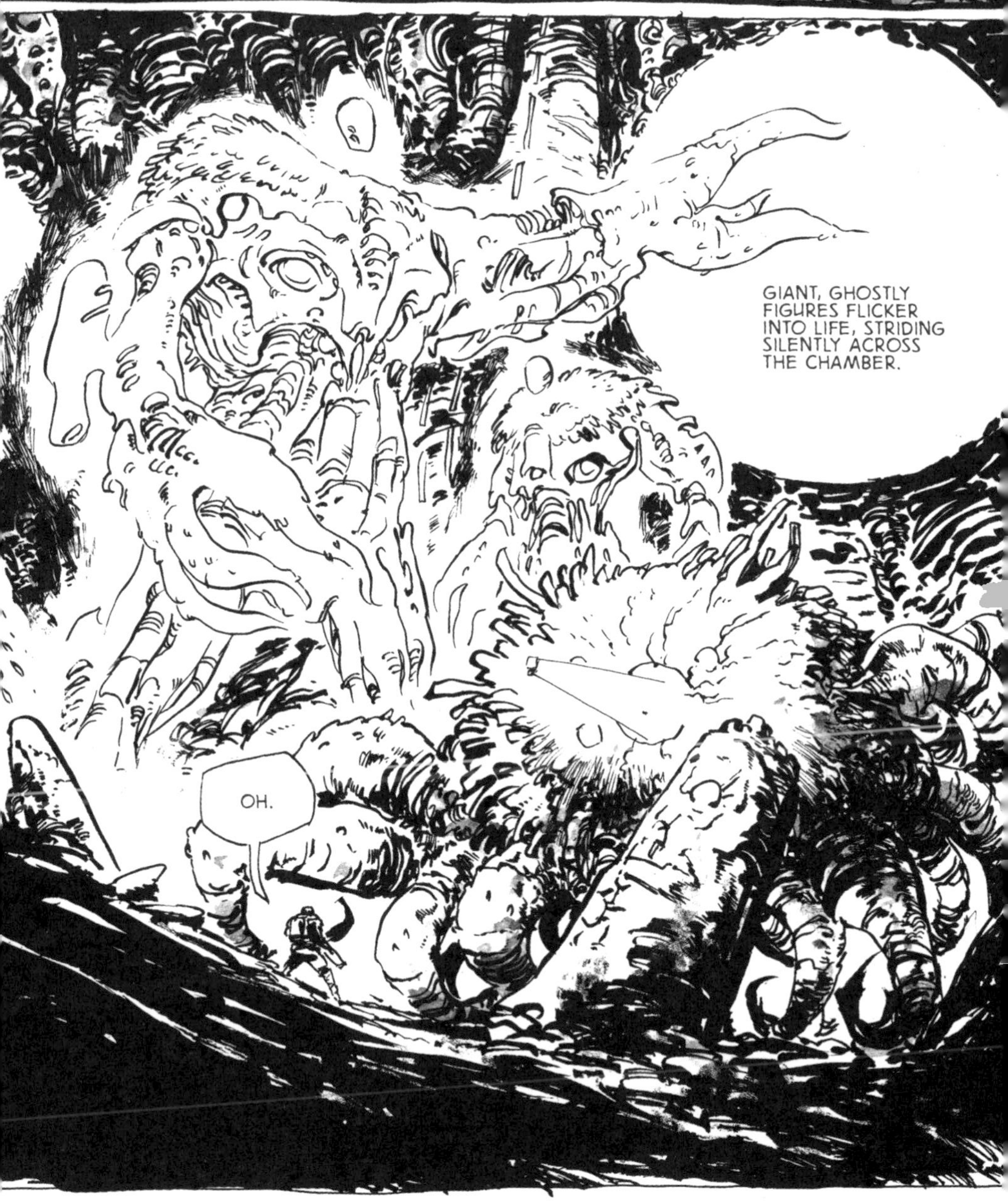
GIANT, GHOSTLY FIGURES FLICKER INTO LIFE, STRIDING SILENTLY ACROSS THE CHAMBER.
OH.

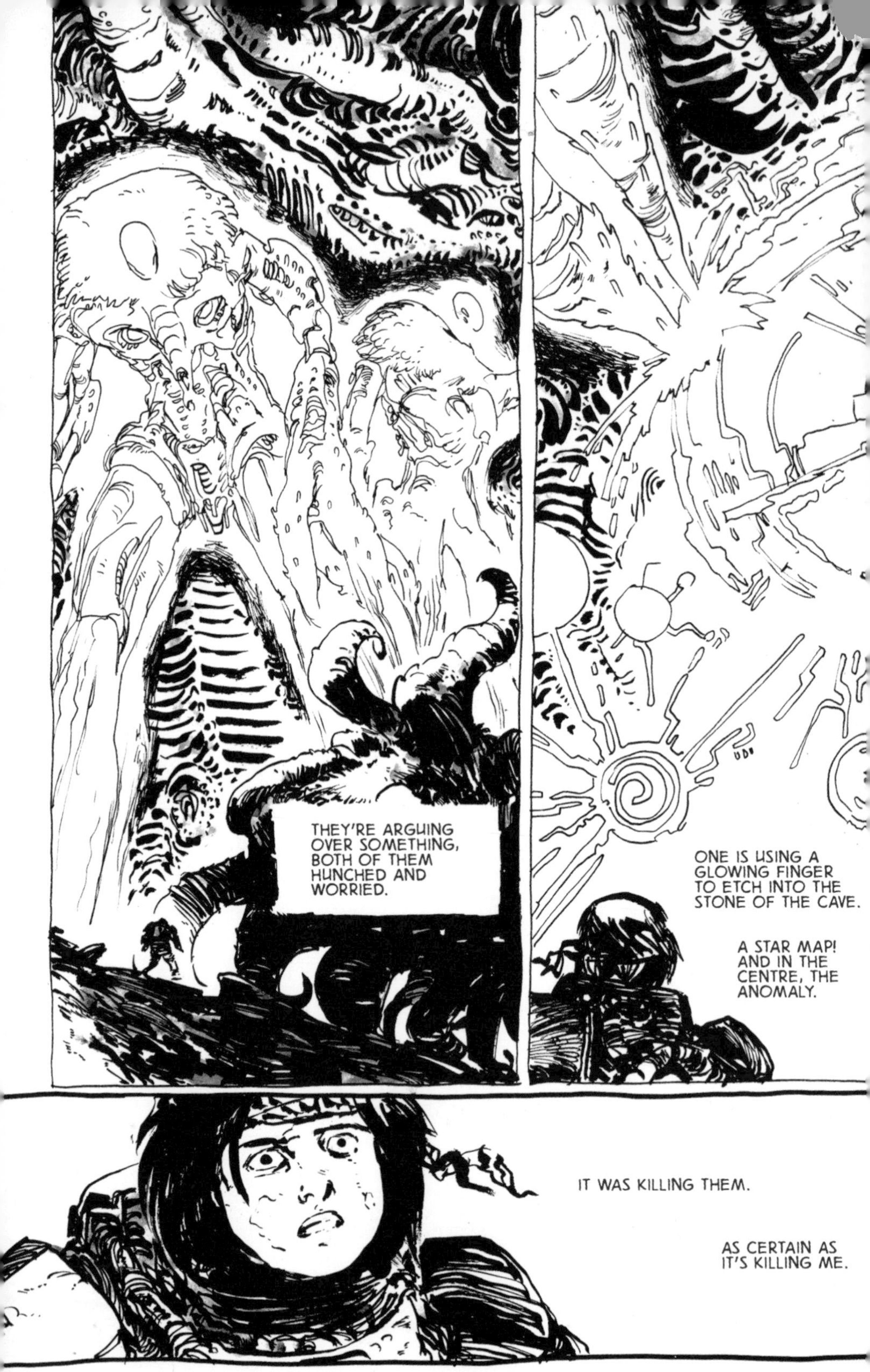
THEY'RE ARGUING OVER SOMETHING, BOTH OF THEM HUNCHED AND WORRIED.
ONE IS USING A GLOWING FINGER TO ETCH INTO THE STONE OF THE CAVE.
A STAR MAP! AND IN THE CENTRE, THE ANOMALY.
IT WAS KILLING THEM.
AS CERTAIN AS IT'S KILLING ME.

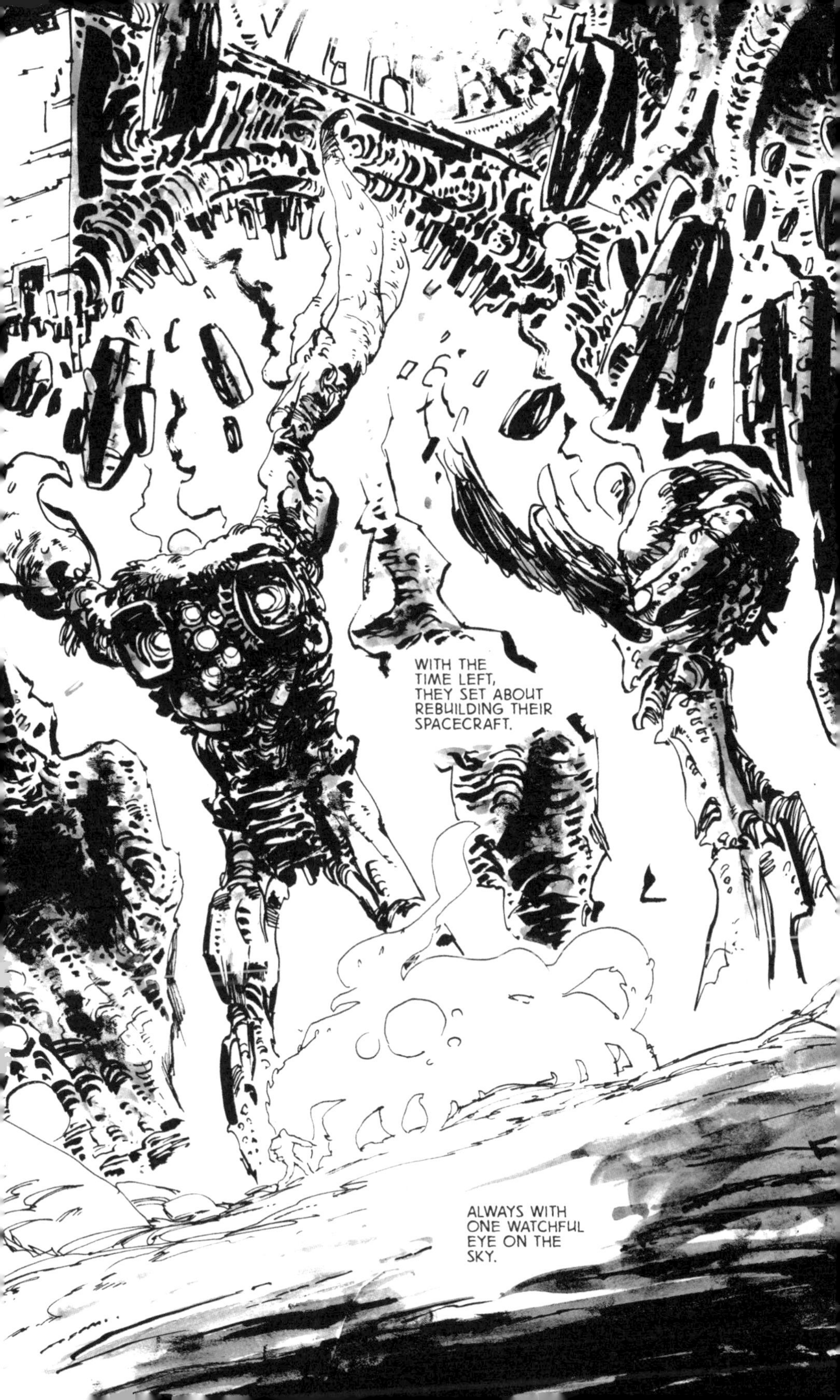
WITH THE
TIME LEFT,
THEY SET ABOUT
REBUILDING THEIR
SPACECRAFT.
ALWAYS WITH
ONE WATCHFUL
EYE ON THE
SKY.

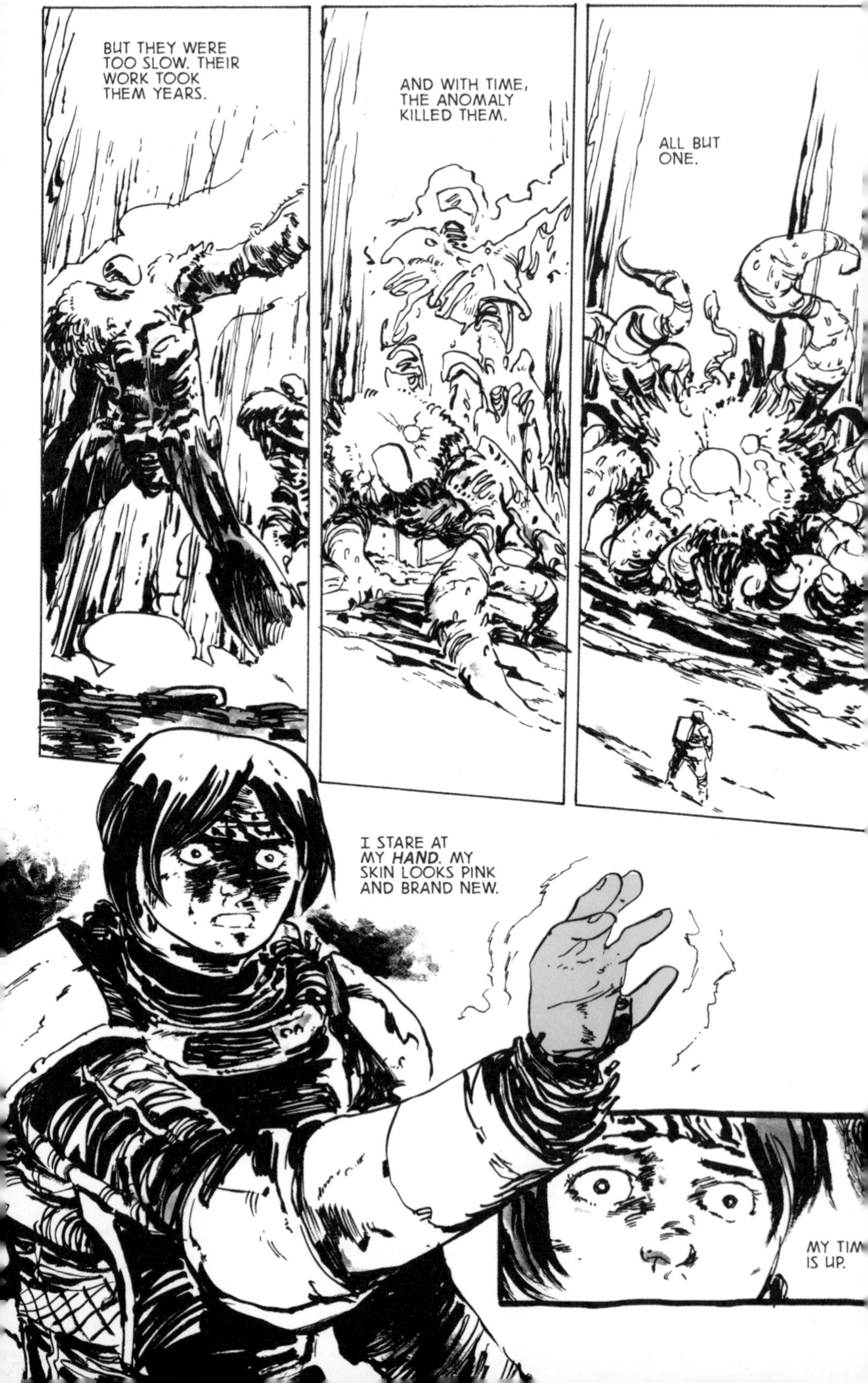
BUT THEY WERE TOO SLOW. THEIR WORK TOOK THEM YEARS.
AND WITH TIME, THE ANOMALY KILLED THEM.
ALL BUT ONE.
I STARE AT MY HAND. MY SKIN LOOKS PINK AND BRAND NEW.
MY TIM
IS UP.

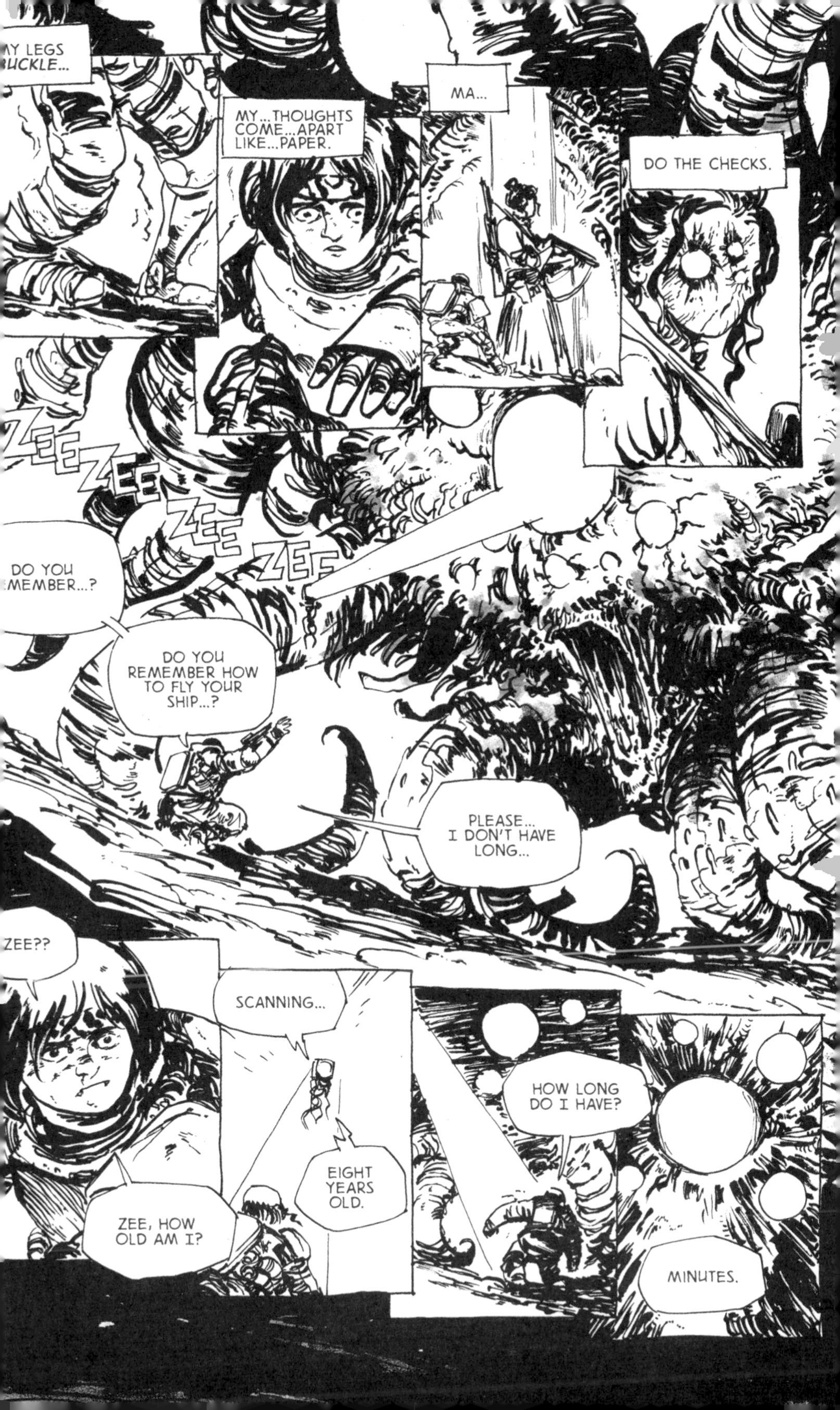
MY LEGS BUCKLE...
MY...THOUGHTS COME...APART LIKE...PAPER.
MA...
DO THE CHECKS.
ZEE ZEE ZEE ZEE
DO YOU REMEMBER...?
DO YOU REMEMBER HOW TO FLY YOUR SHIP...?
PLEASE... I DON'T HAVE LONG...
ZEE??
SCANNING...
ZEE, HOW OLD AM I?
EIGHT YEARS OLD.
HOW LONG DO I HAVE?
MINUTES.

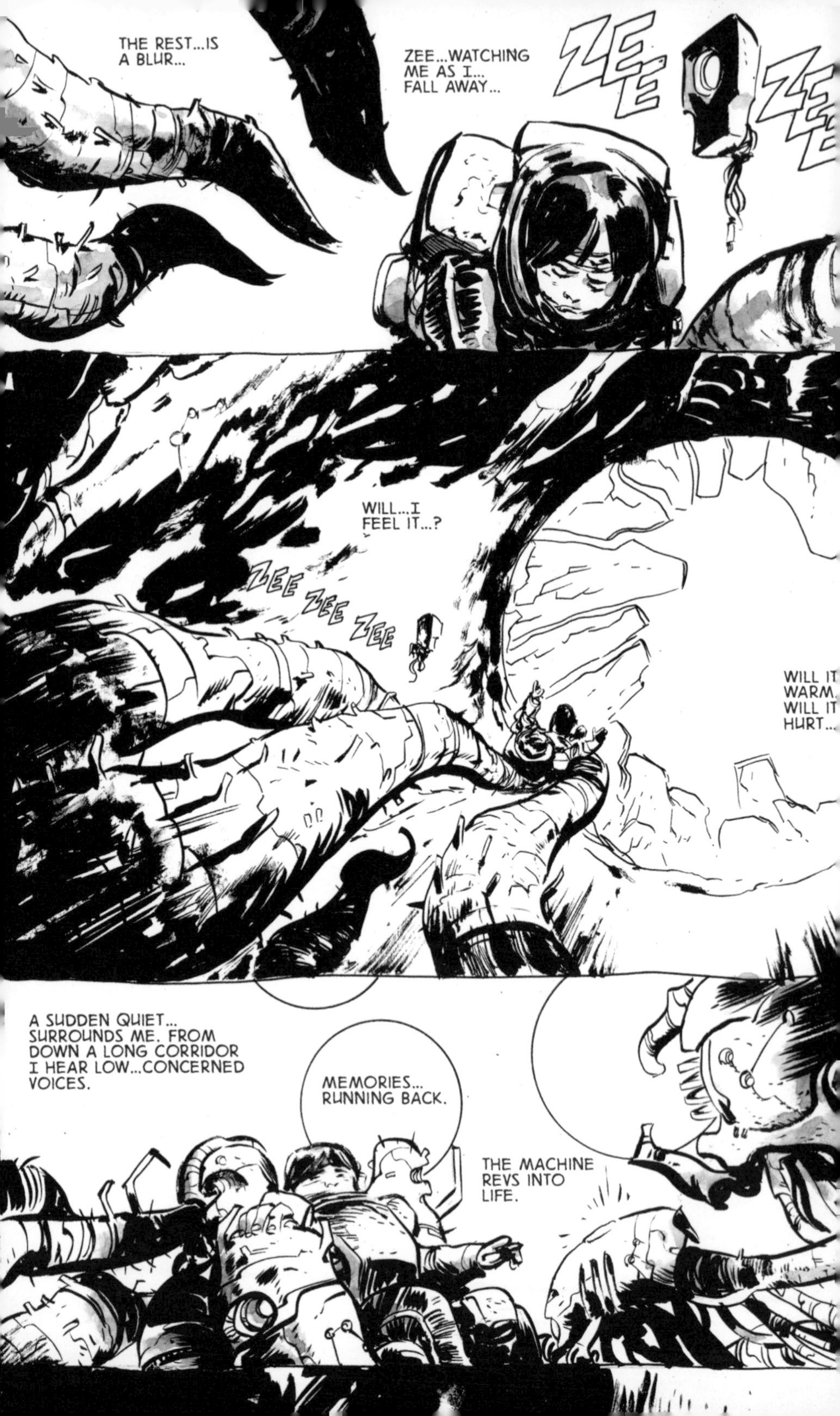
THE REST...IS A BLUR...
ZEE...WATCHING ME AS I... FALL AWAY...
ZEE ZEE
ZEE
WILL...I FEEL IT...?
ZEE ZEE ZEE
WILL IT WARM, WILL IT HURT...
A SUDDEN QUIET... SURROUNDS ME. FROM DOWN A LONG CORRIDOR I HEAR LOW...CONCERNED VOICES.
MEMORIES... RUNNING BACK.
THE MACHINE REVS INTO LIFE.

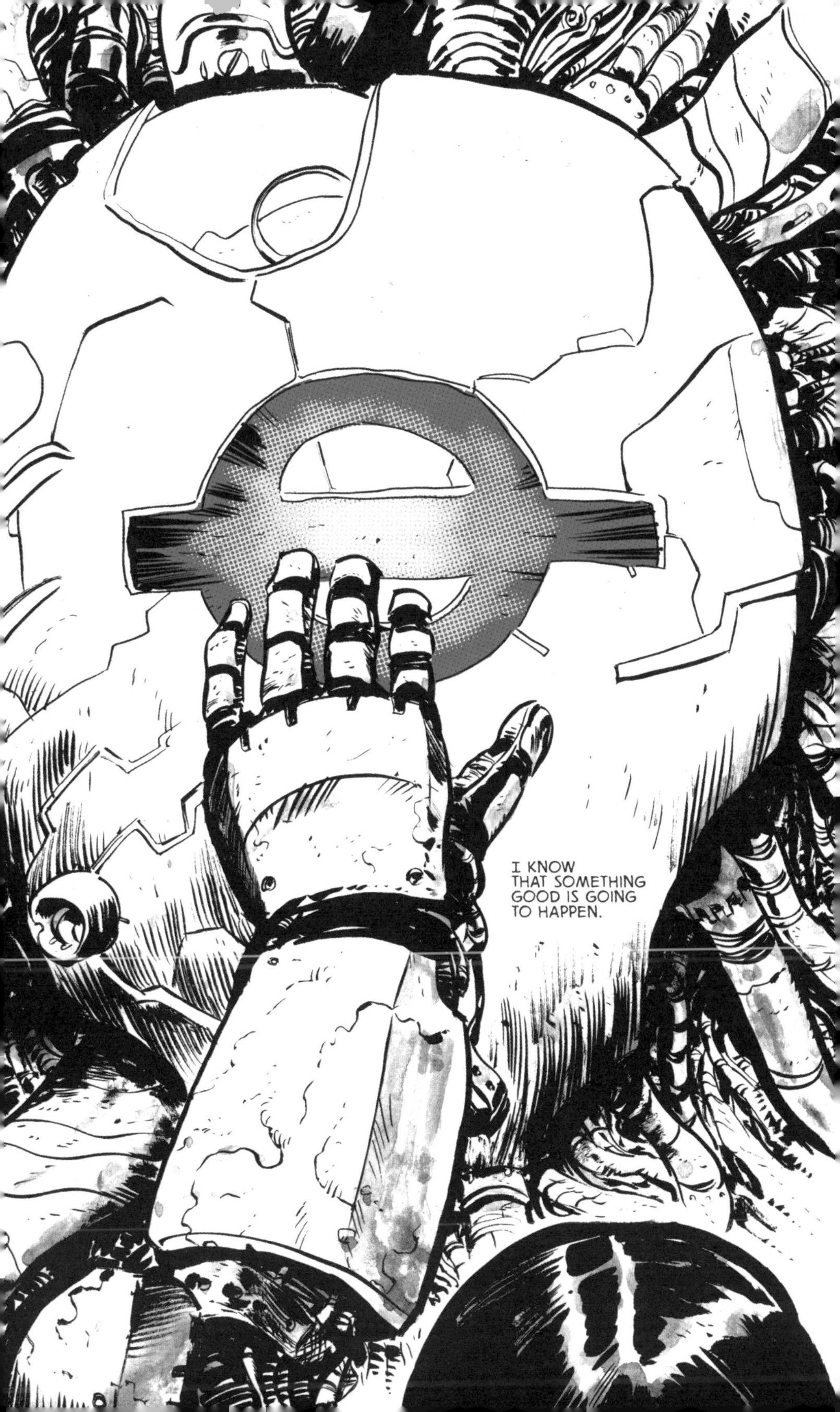
I KNOW THAT SOMETHING GOOD IS GOING TO HAPPEN.

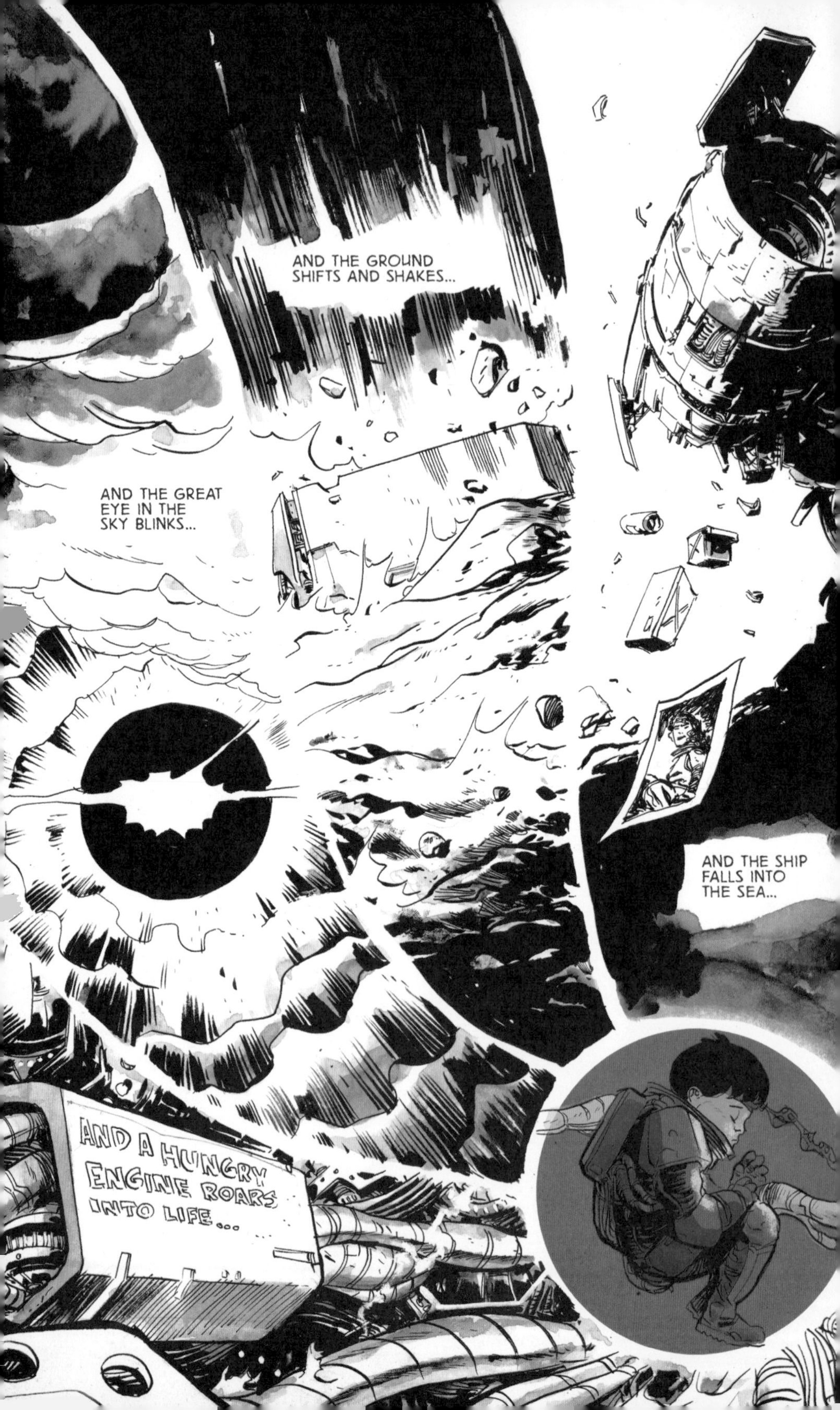
AND THE GROUND SHIFTS AND SHAKES...
AND THE GREAT EYE IN THE SKY BLINKS...
AND THE SHIP FALLS INTO THE SEA...
AND A HUNGRY ENGINE ROARS INTO LIFE...

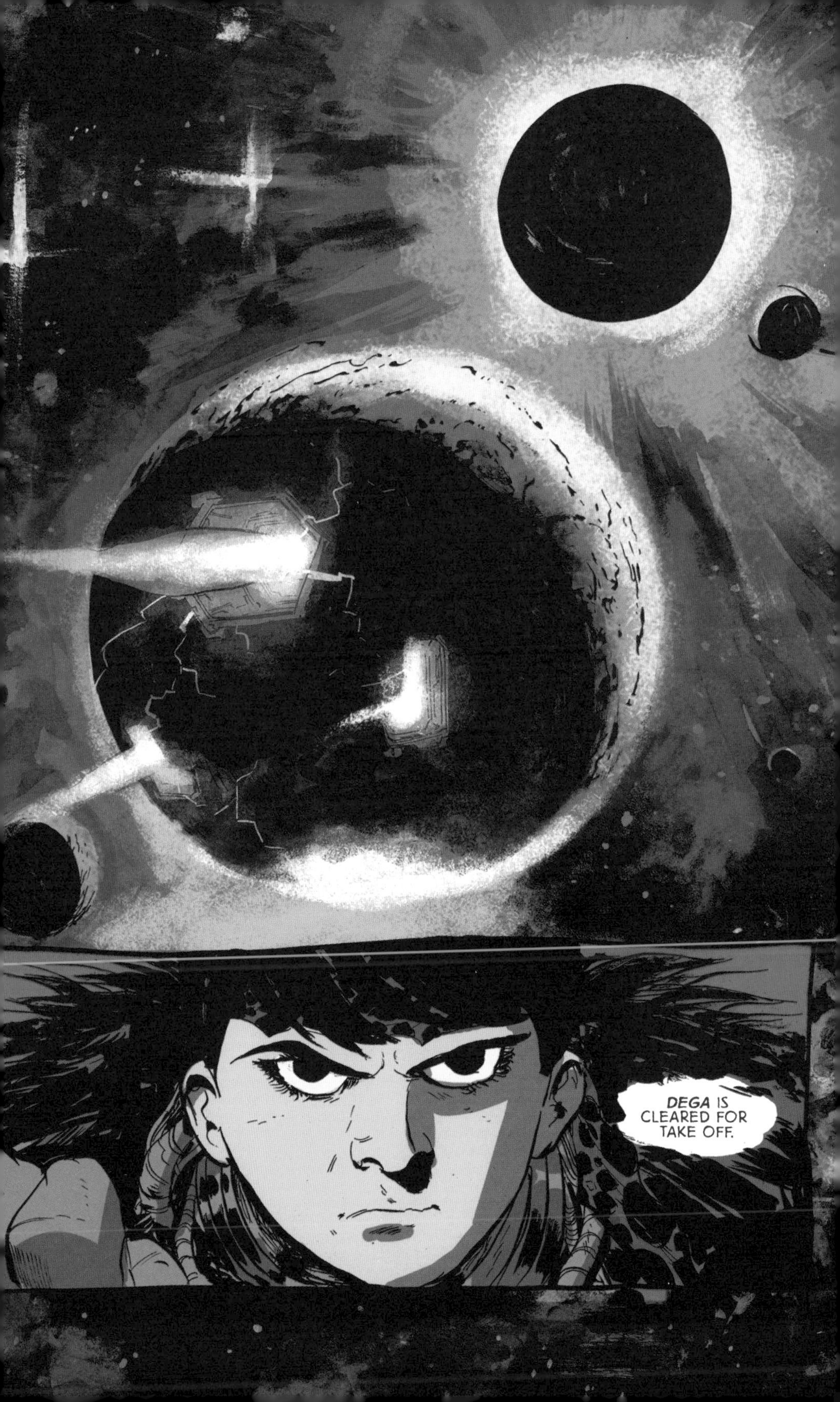
DEGA IS CLEARED FOR TAKE OFF.

DEGA

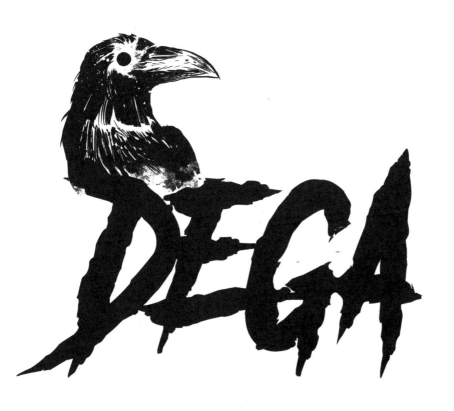

PRODUCTION NOTES

OVER THE NEXT FEW PAGES, YOU'LL SEE THE BEHIND-THE-SCENES PROCESS FOR **DEGA**.

MY USUAL WRITING PROCESS IS TO PLOT, THEN WRITE A FULL SCRIPT FOR MYSELF TO DRAW. I APPROACHED **DEGA** DIFFERENTLY. BECAUSE I WANTED THE TURNAROUND OF THE BOOK TO BE AS FAST AS POSSIBLE, I "WROTE" IT IN THUMBNAIL FORM, WITH NOTES FOR THE DIALOGUE I WANTED ON EACH PAGE. THE IDEA WAS THAT I COULD SKIP THE ONEROUS WRITING PHASE, GET DOWN TO DRAWING FINAL PAGES AS QUICKLY AS POSSIBLE, AND TURN THE WHOLE THING OUT IN ABOUT A MONTH.

IT TOOK CLOSER TO FIVE YEARS.

THE PAGES AHEAD ARE A BIT OF A SCRABBLE OF NOISE AND NONSENSE, NOTES THAT MIGHT ONLY MAKE SENSE TO ME. BUT I KNOW SOME OF YOU WEIRDOS LIKE THAT SORT OF THING— GOD KNOWS I DO—SO HERE IT IS.

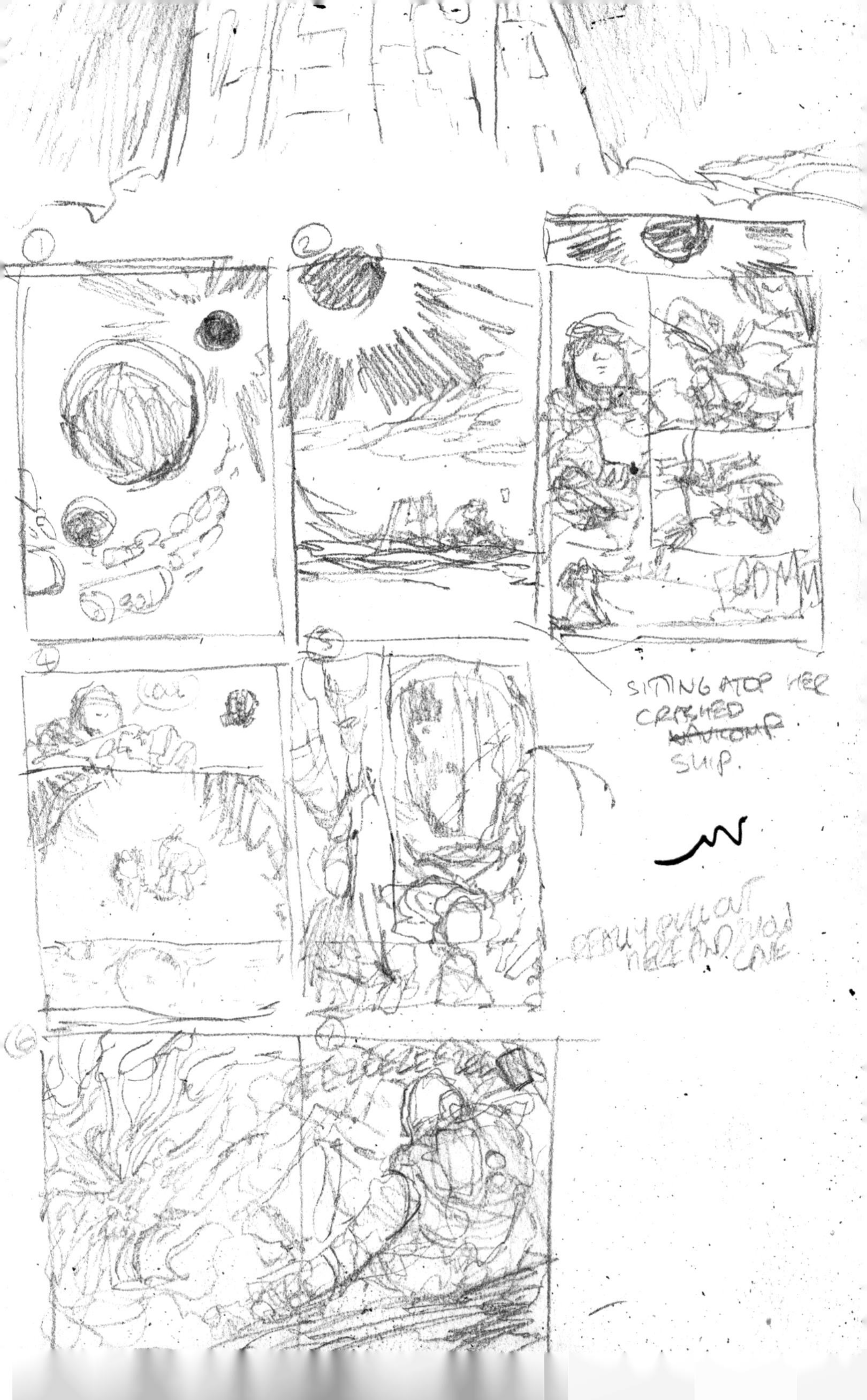
SITTING ATOP HER CRASHED ~~NAVCOMP~~ SHIP.

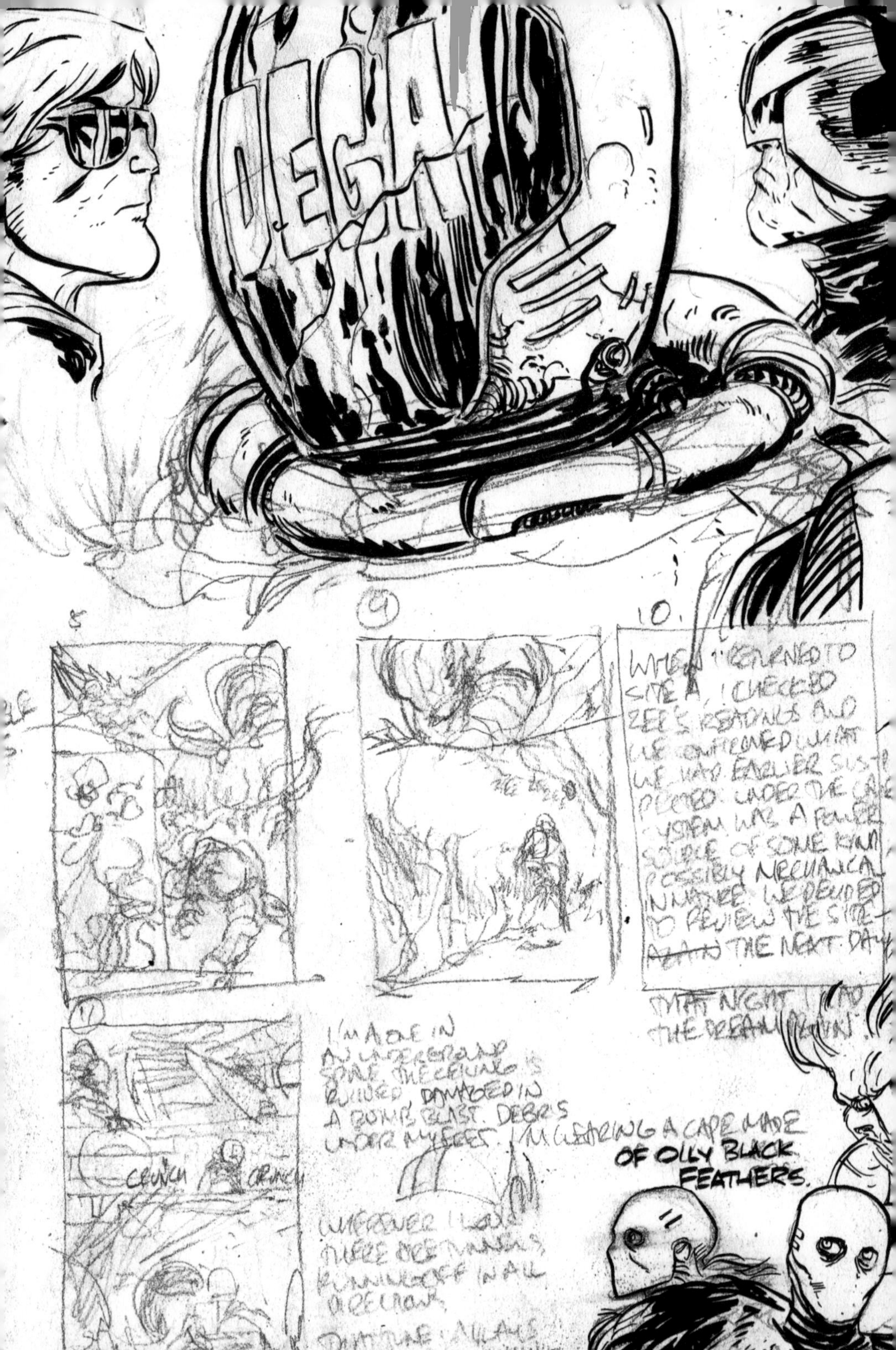
9
10.
I'M ALONE IN
A BOMB BLAST. DEBRIS
OF OLLY BLACK
FEATHERS.
11
CRUNCH
CRUNCH

AS YOU CAN TELL FROM THIS PAGE, IT'S AROUND THIS POINT THAT I STARTED WORK ON THE JUDGE DREDD COMIC FOR IDW.

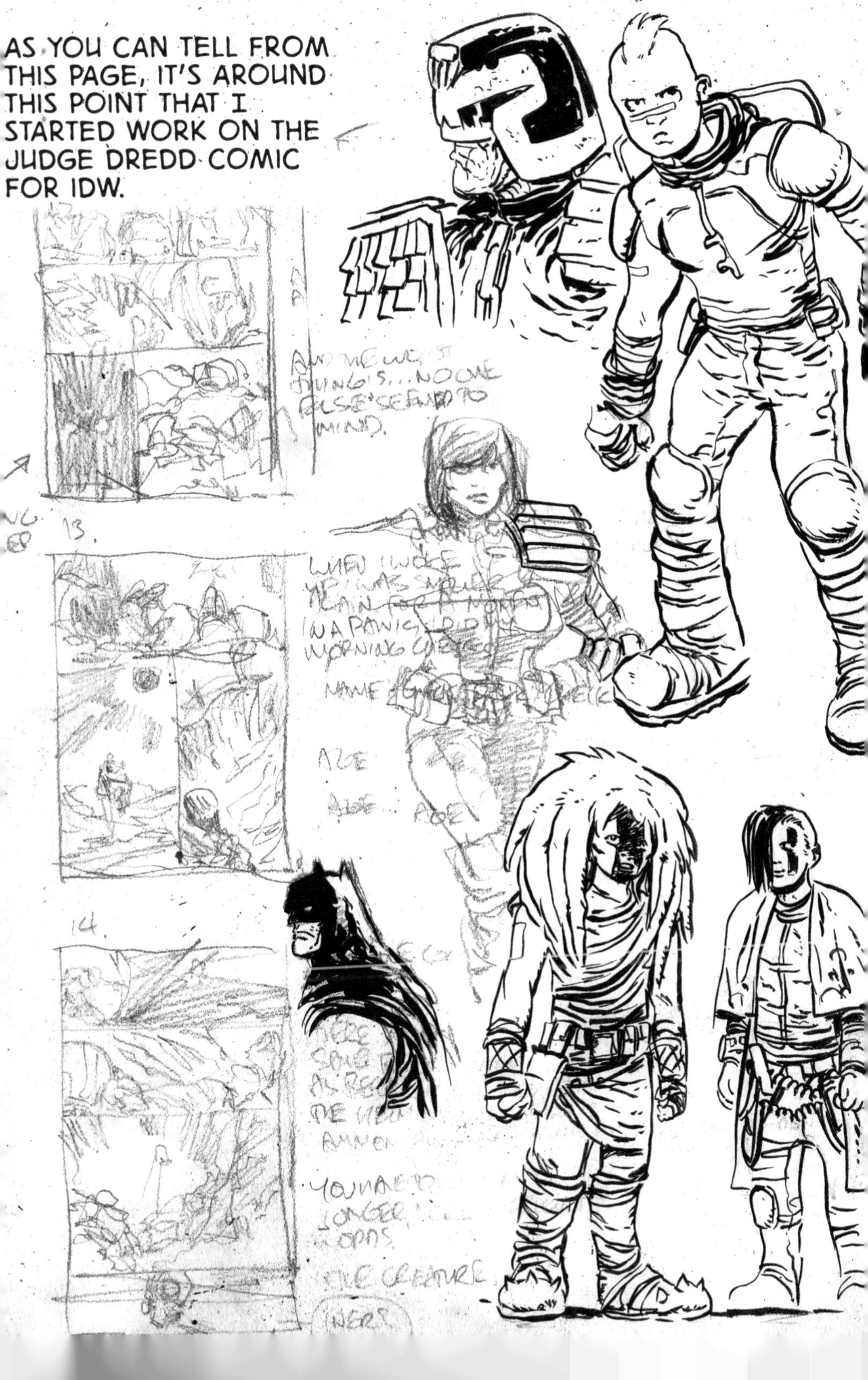

15.

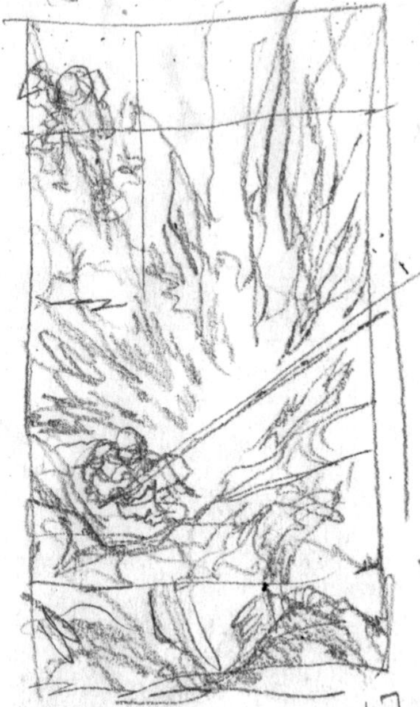

GOOD, BUT TRY NO [illegible]
LIGHT [illegible]

~~THEN I SEE~~
DOWN WE GO

19.

ZZNOT

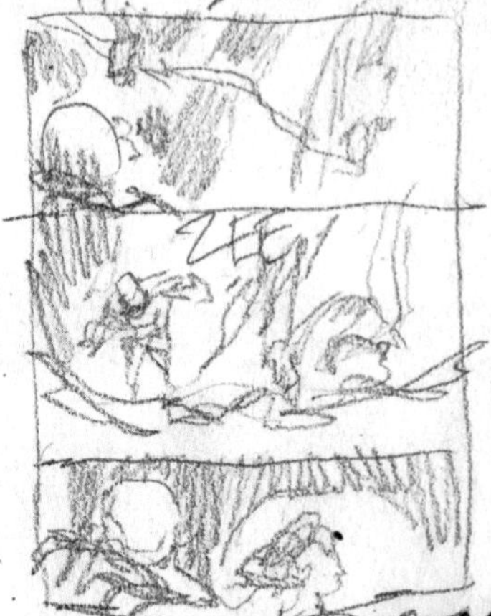
ZEE

THEN I SEE IT.

THE LIGHTS GO
I SUDDENLY
FEEL W

16 17.

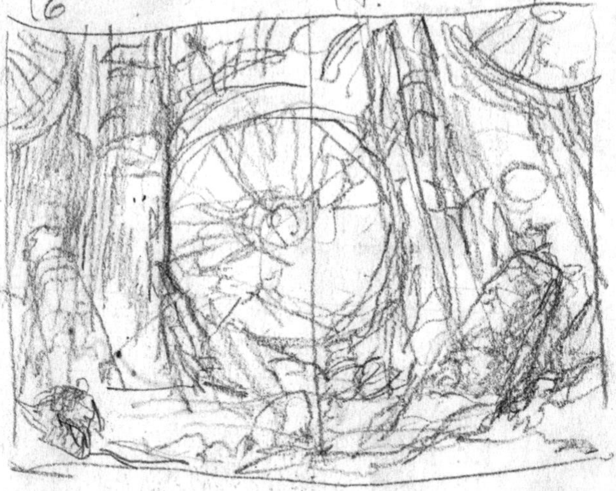

MACHINERY
OR SOMETHING
LIKE IT

A MECHANICAL
CATHEDRAL! VAST
IN SCALE!

18

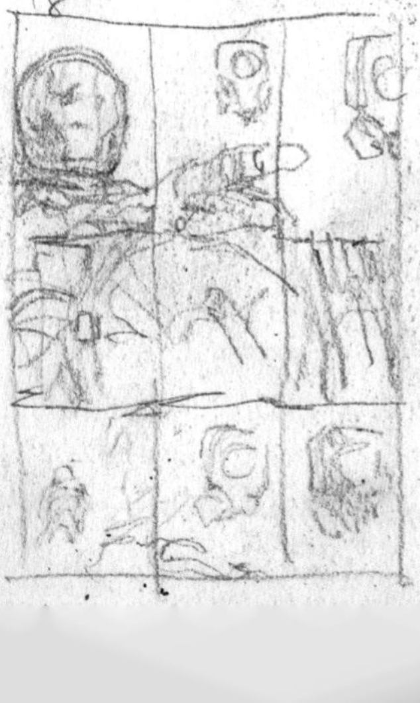

ZEE...
~~CONTACT~~
CONFIRMED. ENERGY
SOURCE CONFIRMED.
ANALYSING.

ZEE ZEE ZEE

ZEE ZZ-
CONTACT
CONTACT
CONTACT

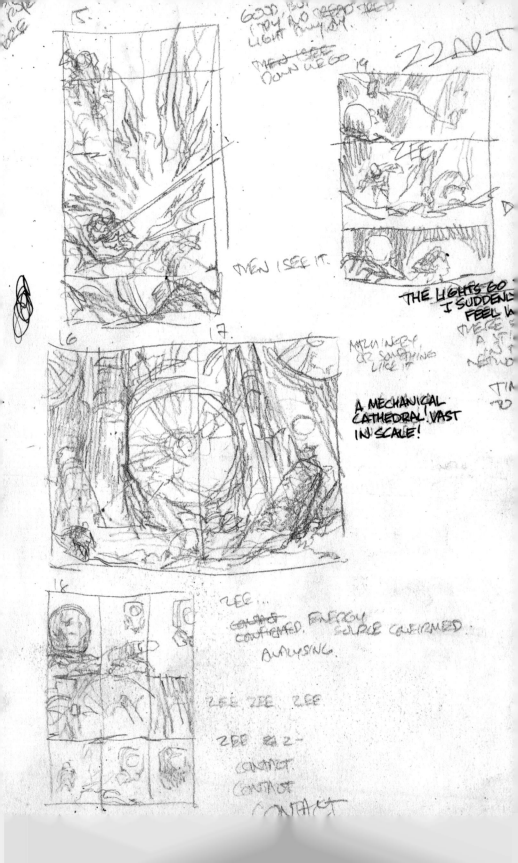

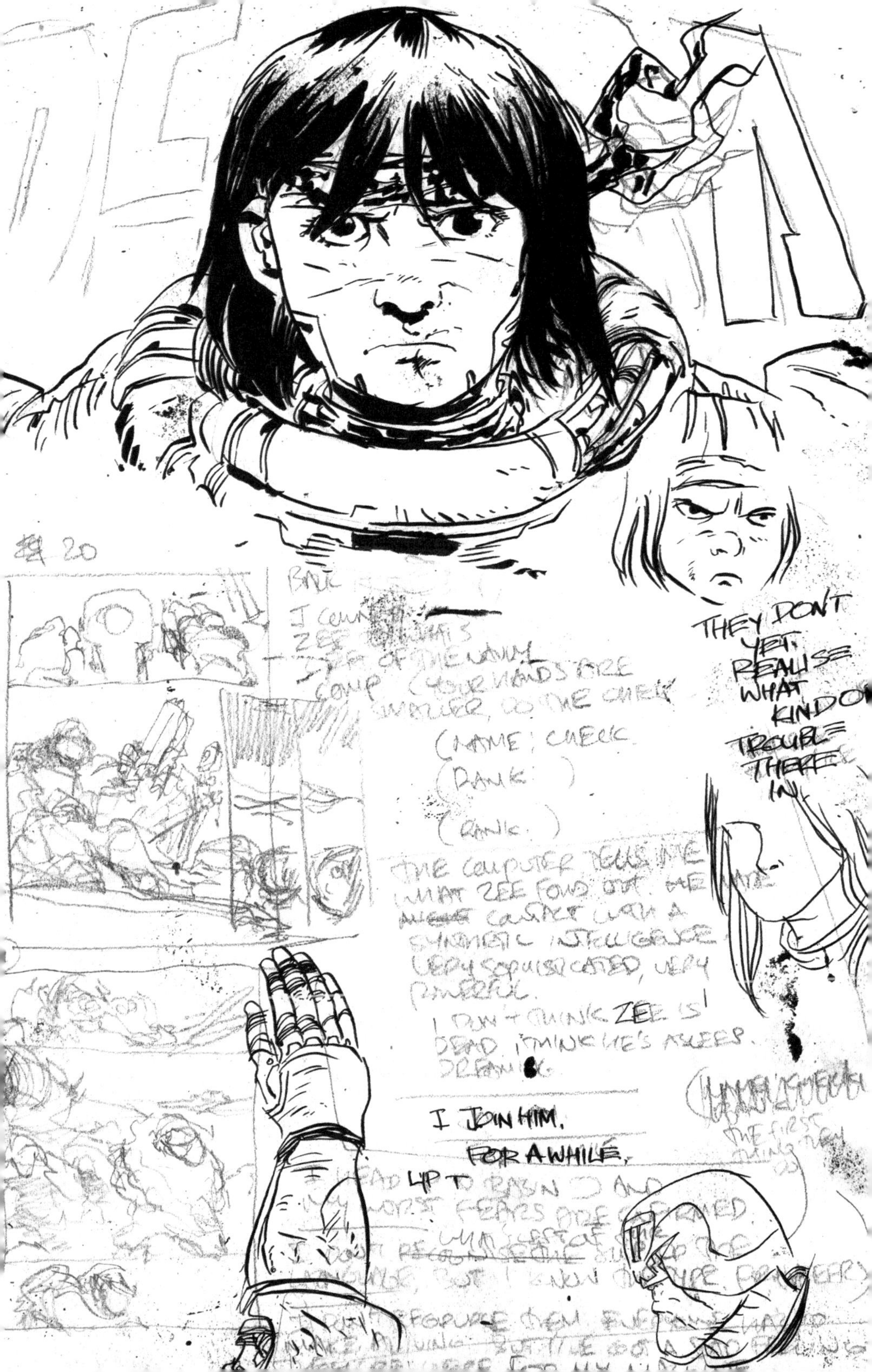

(NAME: CHECK
(RANK
I JOIN HIM.
FOR A WHILE.

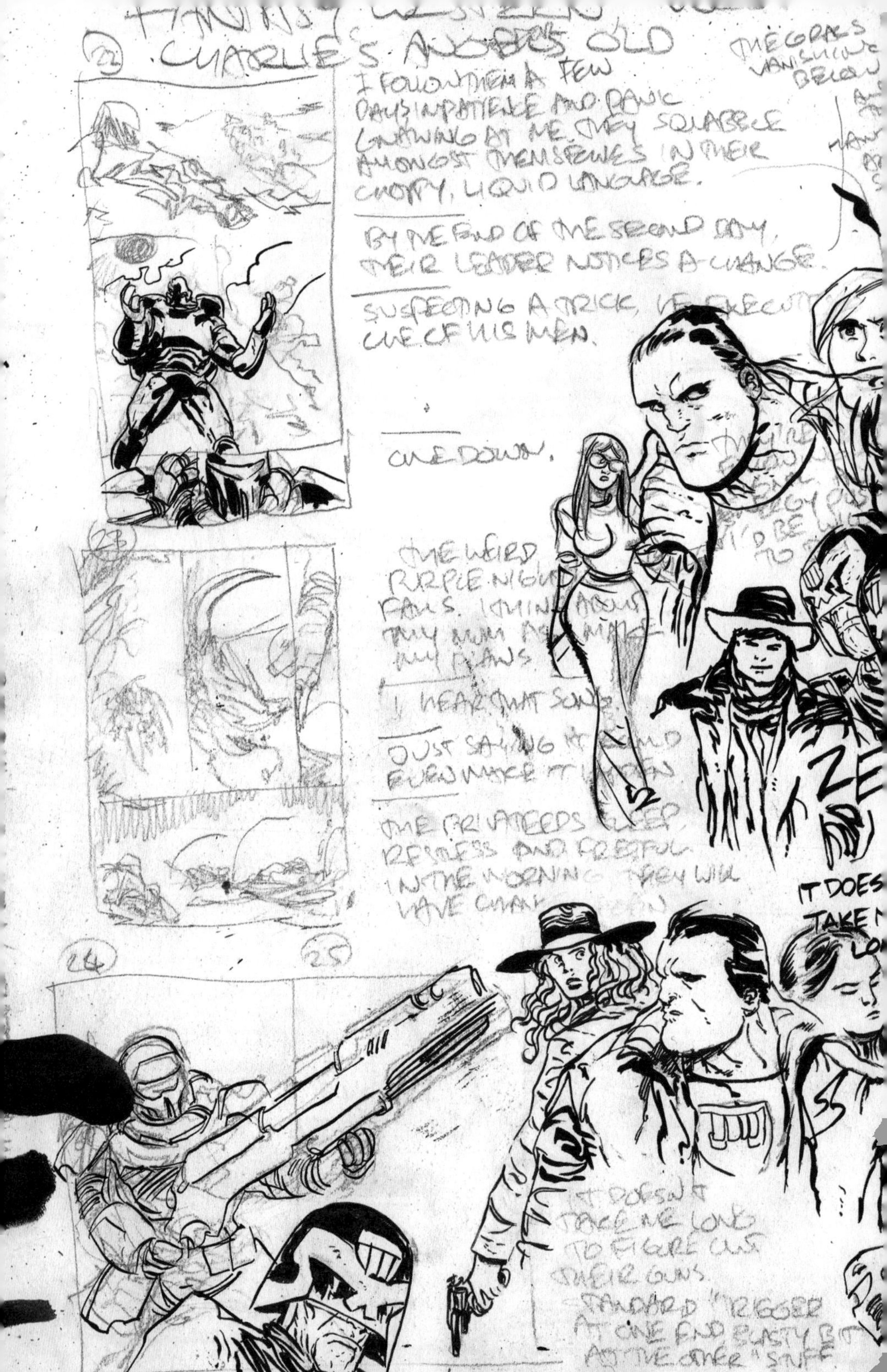
I FOLLOW THEM A FEW DAYS IMPATIENCE AND PANIC GNAWING AT ME. THEY SQUABBLE AMONGST THEMSELVES IN THEIR CHOPPY, LIQUID LANGUAGE.
BY THE END OF THE SECOND DAY, THEIR LEADER NOTICES A CHANGE.
SUSPECTING A TRICK,
ONE OF HIS MEN.
ONE DOWN.
THE WEIRD PURPLE NIGHT FALLS.
I HEAR THAT SONG.
THE PRIVATEERS SLEEP RESTLESS AND FRETFUL.
IT DOESN'T TAKE ME LONG TO FIGURE OUT THEIR GUNS.
STANDARD "TRIGGER AT ONE END BLASTY BIT AT THE OTHER" STUFF
(NAME. RANK.

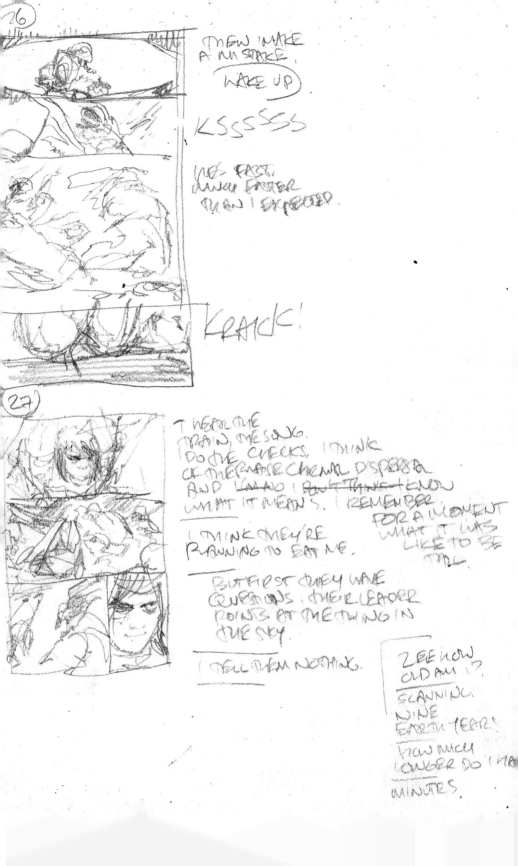

26

THEN I MAKE
A MISTAKE.

(WAKE UP)

KSSSSSS

IT'S FAST.
MUCH FASTER
THAN I EXPECTED.

KRAK!

27

I HEAR THE
BRAIN, THE SONG.
I DO THE CHECKS, I THINK
OF THE FLAVOR CHEMICAL DISPERSAL
AND I— AND I DON'T THINK I KNOW
WHAT IT MEANS. I REMEMBER
FOR A MOMENT
WHAT IT WAS
LIKE TO BE
TALL.

I THINK THEY'RE
PLANNING TO EAT ME.

BUT FIRST THEY HAVE
QUESTIONS. THEIR LEADER
POINTS AT THE THING IN
THE SKY.

I TELL THEM NOTHING.

ZEE HOW
OLD AM I?

SCANNING.
NINE
EARTH YEARS

HOW MUCH
LONGER DO I HAVE

MINUTES.

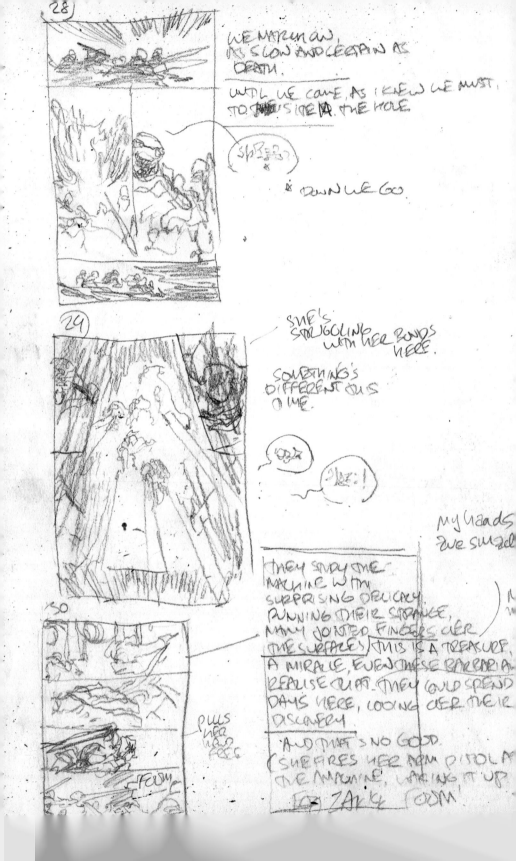

28

WE MARCH ON,
AS SLOW AND CERTAIN AS
DEATH.

UNTIL WE CAME, AS I KNEW WE MUST,
TO ~~THIS~~ SIDE OF THE HOLE

SPEECH?

* DOWN WE GO

29

SHE'S
STRUGGLING
WITH HER BONDS
HERE.

SOMETHING'S
DIFFERENT THIS
TIME.

MY HANDS
ARE SWEAT-

SO

THEY STUDY THE
MACHINE WITH
SURPRISING DELICACY,
RUNNING THEIR STRANGE,
MANY-JOINTED FINGERS OVER
THE SURFACES. THIS IS A TREASURE,
A MIRACLE, EVEN THESE BARBARIA-
REALISE THAT. THEY COULD SPEND
DAYS HERE, LOOKING OVER THEIR
DISCOVERY

PULLS
HER
HAND
FREE

AND THAT'S NO GOOD.
SHE FIRES HER ARM PISTOL A-
THE MACHINE, WAKING IT UP.

FOOM

FOR ZARK' FOOM!

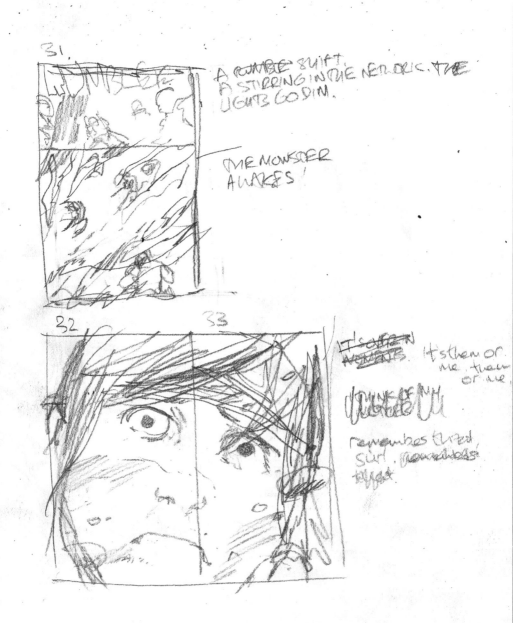

31.

A RUMBLE SHIFT.
A STIRRING IN THE NETLORK. THE
LIGHTS GO DIM.

THE MONSTER
AWAKES!

32. 33.

~~It's often~~
~~Always~~. It's them or
me. them
or me.

~~I think of my~~
~~lifetime~~

remembers Elzel,
Surf. ~~remembers~~
~~Elzel.~~

P.J.O.▷▷▷

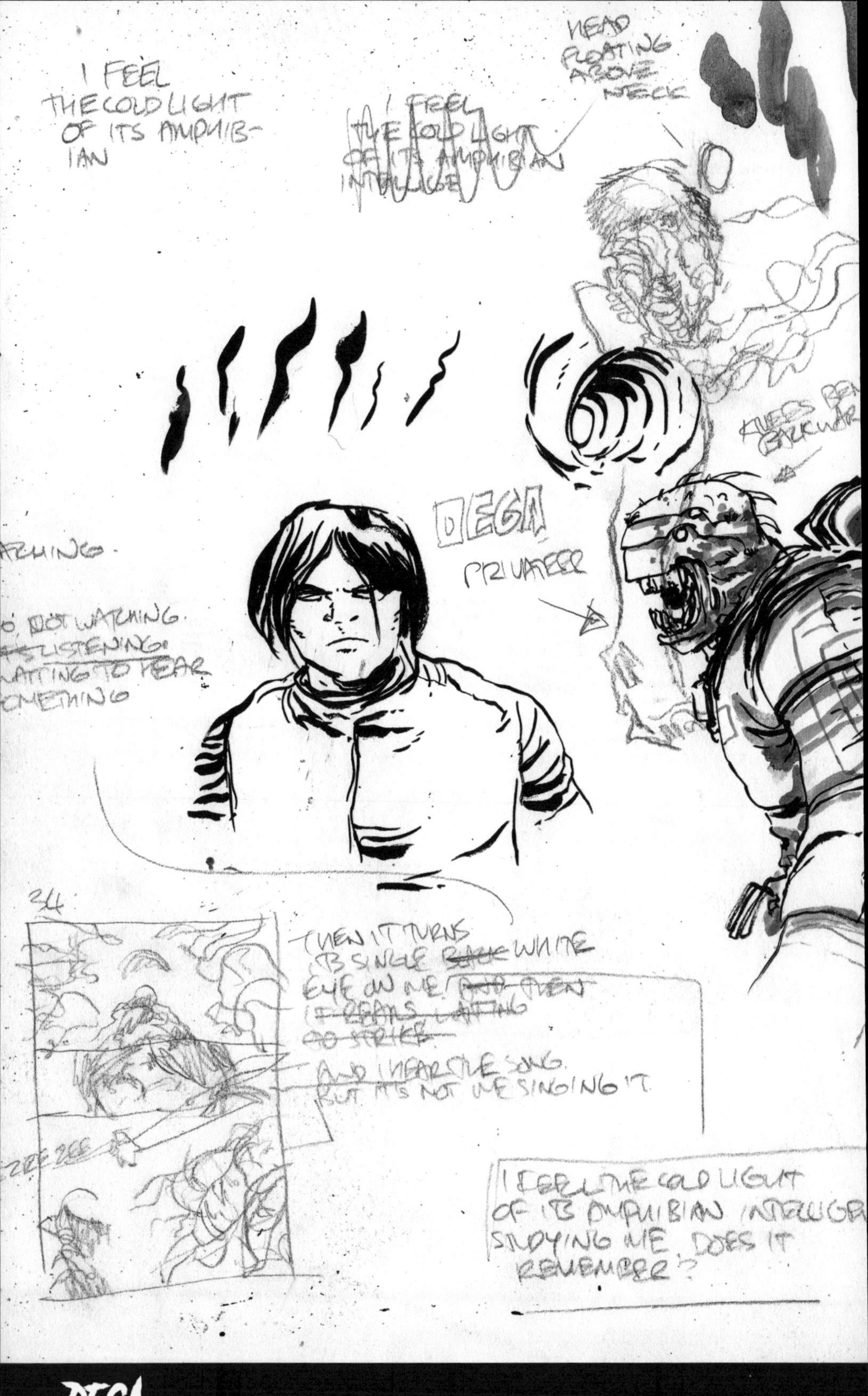
I FEEL THE COLD LIGHT OF ITS AMPHIB-IAN
HEAD FLOATING ABOVE NECK
DEGA
PRIVATEER
NOT WATCHING.
WAITING TO HEAR
34
THEN IT TURNS ITS SINGLE WHITE EYE ON ME
AND I HEAR THE SONG. BUT IT'S NOT ME SINGING IT.
I FEEL THE COLD LIGHT OF ITS AMPHIBIAN STUDYING ME. DOES IT REMEMBER?

35

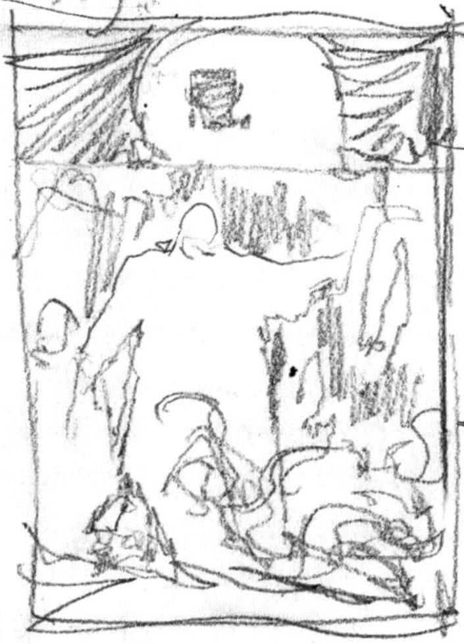

CONTACT.

GIANT, GHOSTLY FIGURES FLICKER INTO LIFE, STRIDING SILENTLY ACROSS THE CHAMBER.

DESCRIBING A MACHINE WITH LIGHT. NO... BUILDING ONE.

36.

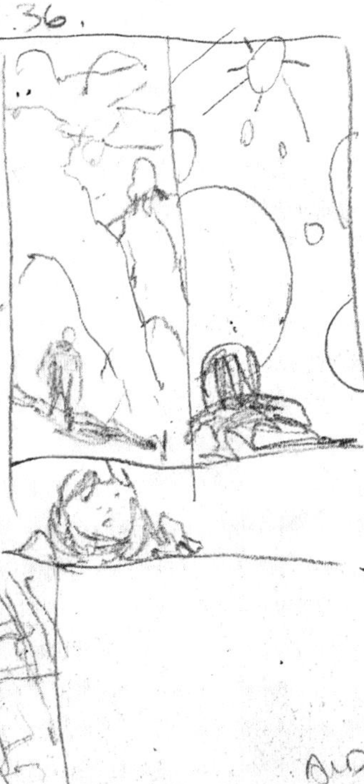

THEY'RE ARGUING OVER SOMETHING I REALISE, BOTH OF THEM HUNCHED AND WORRIED. ~~[illegible]~~

ONE IS USING A GLOWING FINGER TO BURN INTO THE STONE OF THE CAVE

A STAR MAP! A CELESTIAL ANOMALY

IT WAS KILLING THEM.

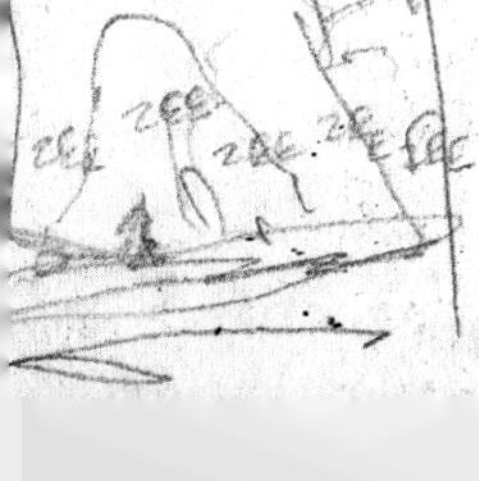

ZEE ZEE ZEE ZEE ZEE

AND

WITH THE TIME LEFT THEY BUILT A SHIP. A MECHANICAL MARVEL THE SIZE OF A WORLD. A GUARDIAN, TO PROTECT THEIR WORK.

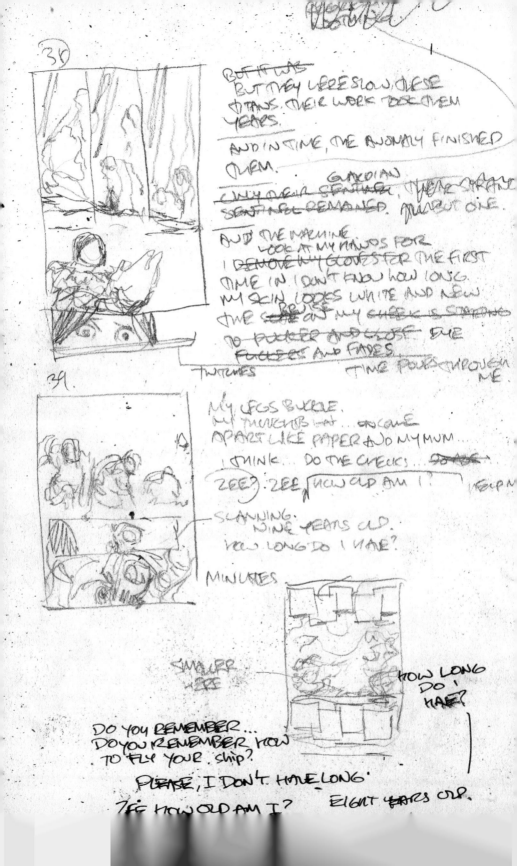

38

BUT IT WAS
BUT THEY WERE SLOW, THESE
TITANS. THEIR WORK TOOK THEM
YEARS.
AND IN TIME, THE ANOMALY FINISHED
THEM.
GUARDIAN
~~ONLY THEIR SENTINEL~~ THEIR STRANGE
~~SENTINEL REMAINED.~~ ALL BUT ONE.

AND THE MACHINE
LOOK AT MY HANDS FOR
I ~~REMOVE~~ MY GLOVES FOR THE FIRST
TIME IN I DON'T KNOW HOW LONG.
MY SKIN LOOKS WHITE AND NEW
THE ~~SCAR~~ ON MY ~~CHEEK IS STARTING~~
TO ~~PUCKER AND CLOSE~~ EYE
~~PUCKERS~~ AND FADES.
TWITCHES   TIME POURS THROUGH ME

39

MY LEGS BUCKLE.
MY THOUGHTS ~~HAT~~ ... ON COME
APART LIKE PAPER AND MY MUM ...
I THINK ... DO THE CHECKS ... ~~DO THE~~
ZEE? ZEE, HOW OLD AM I?   KELP M

SCANNING.
NINE YEARS OLD.
HOW LONG DO I HAVE?

MINUTES

SMALLER
+FIT

HOW LONG
DO I
HAVE?

DO YOU REMEMBER ...
DO YOU REMEMBER HOW
TO FLY YOUR . SHIP?

PLEASE, I DON'T HAVE LONG.
ZEE HOW OLD AM I?   EIGHT YEARS OLD.

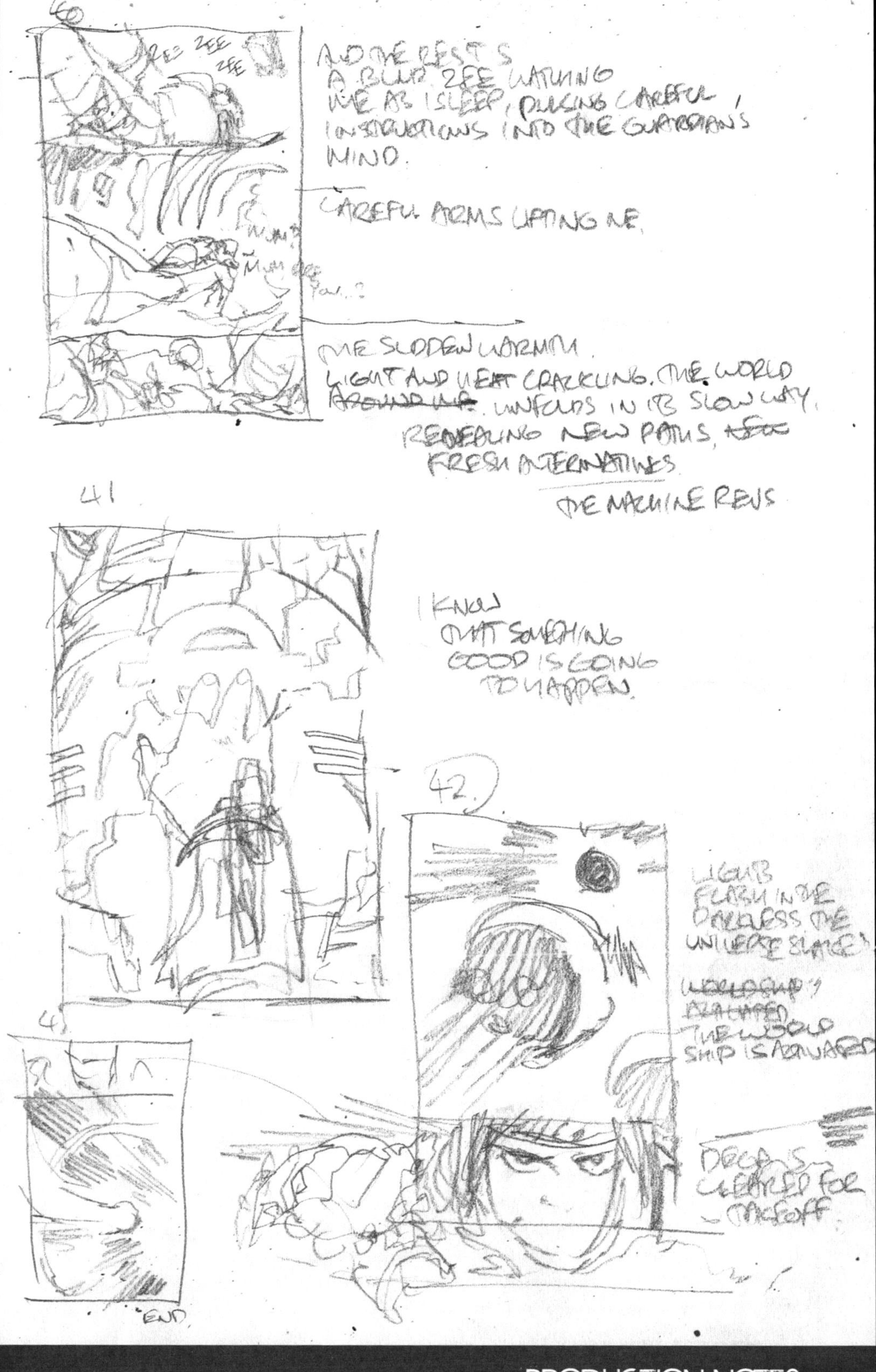
40
AND THE REST'S A BLUR. ZEE WATCHING ME AS I SLEEP, PULSING CAREFUL INSTRUCTIONS INTO THE GUARDIAN'S MIND.
CAREFUL ARMS LIFTING ME.
THE SUDDEN WARMTH
LIGHT AND HEAT CRACKLING. THE WORLD ~~AROUND ME~~ UNFOLDS IN ITS SLOW WAY, REVEALING NEW PATHS, FRESH ALTERNATIVES
THE MACHINE REVS
41
I KNOW THAT SOMETHING GOOD IS GOING TO HAPPEN.
42.
DECA IS CLEARED FOR TAKEOFF
END

ORIGINAL DESIGN FOR THE
LEAD CHARACTER. IN THE END,
I WENT SOMETHING A LITTLE
SCUZZIER, MORE AD HOC.

DEGAAGED

by DAN McDAID

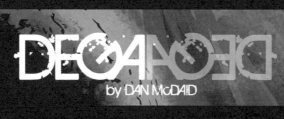

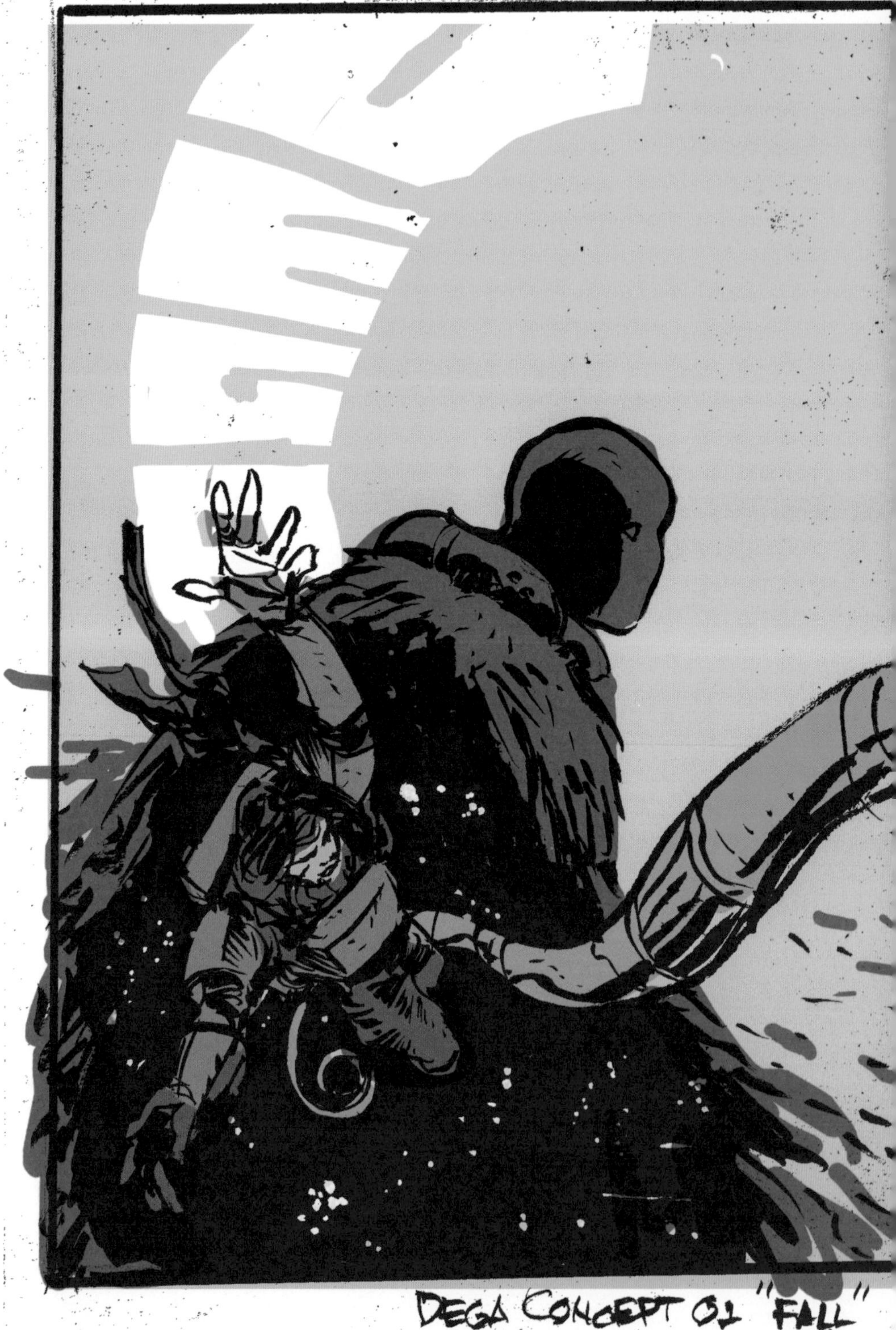

DEGA CONCEPT 01 "FALL"

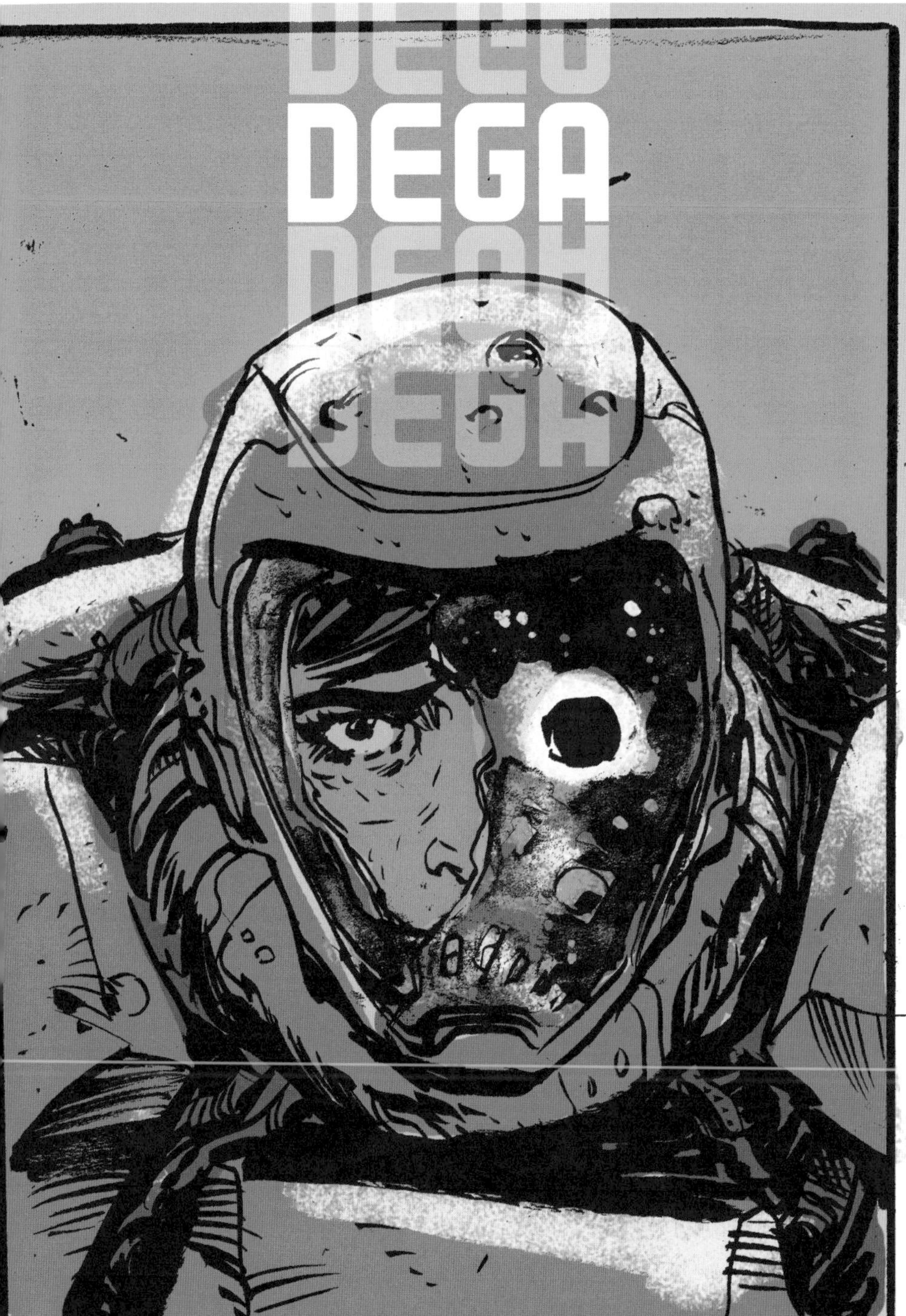
DEGA

DEGA CONCEPT 02- "SKULL"

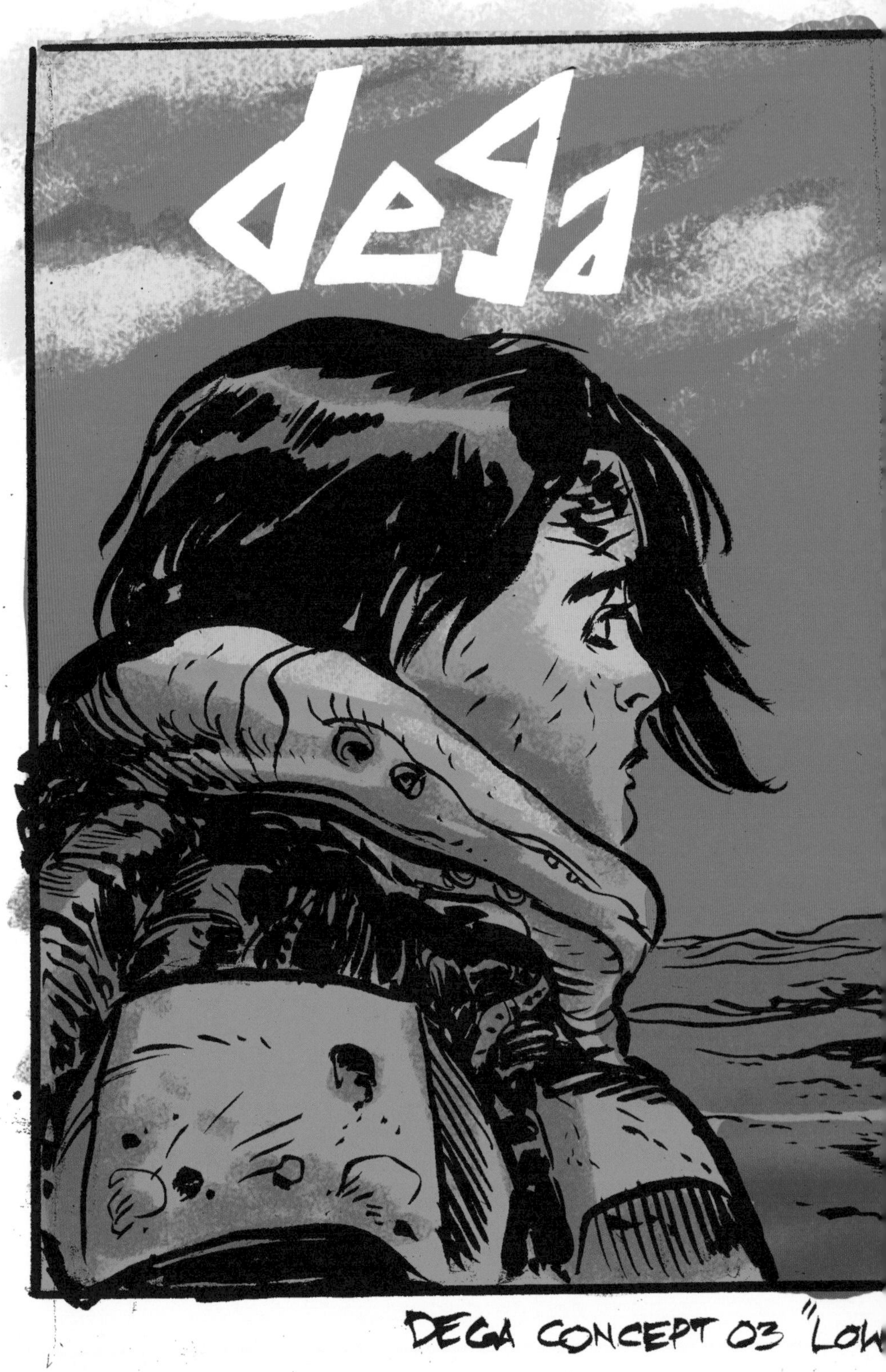
dega

DEGA CONCEPT 03 "LOW

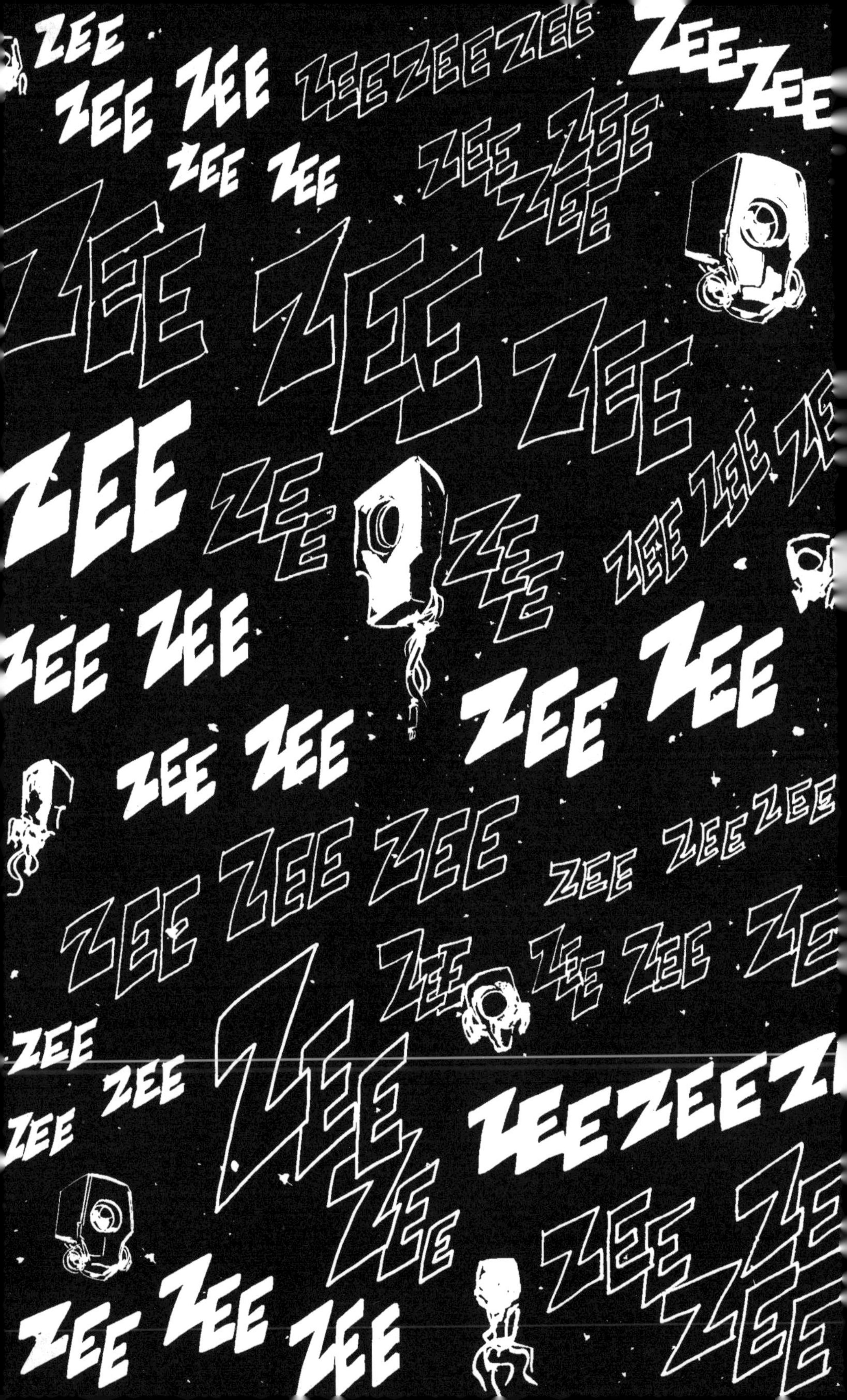
ZEE ZEE ZEE ZEE ZEE ZEE ZEE
ZEE ZEE ZEE
ZEE ZEE
ZEE ZEE ZEE
ZEE ZEE ZEE ZEE ZEE
ZEE ZEE ZEE ZEE
ZEE ZEE ZEE ZEE ZEE ZEE
ZEE ZEE ZEE ZEE ZEE ZEE
ZEE ZEE ZEE ZEE ZEE
ZEE ZEE ZEE ZEE ZEE ZEE

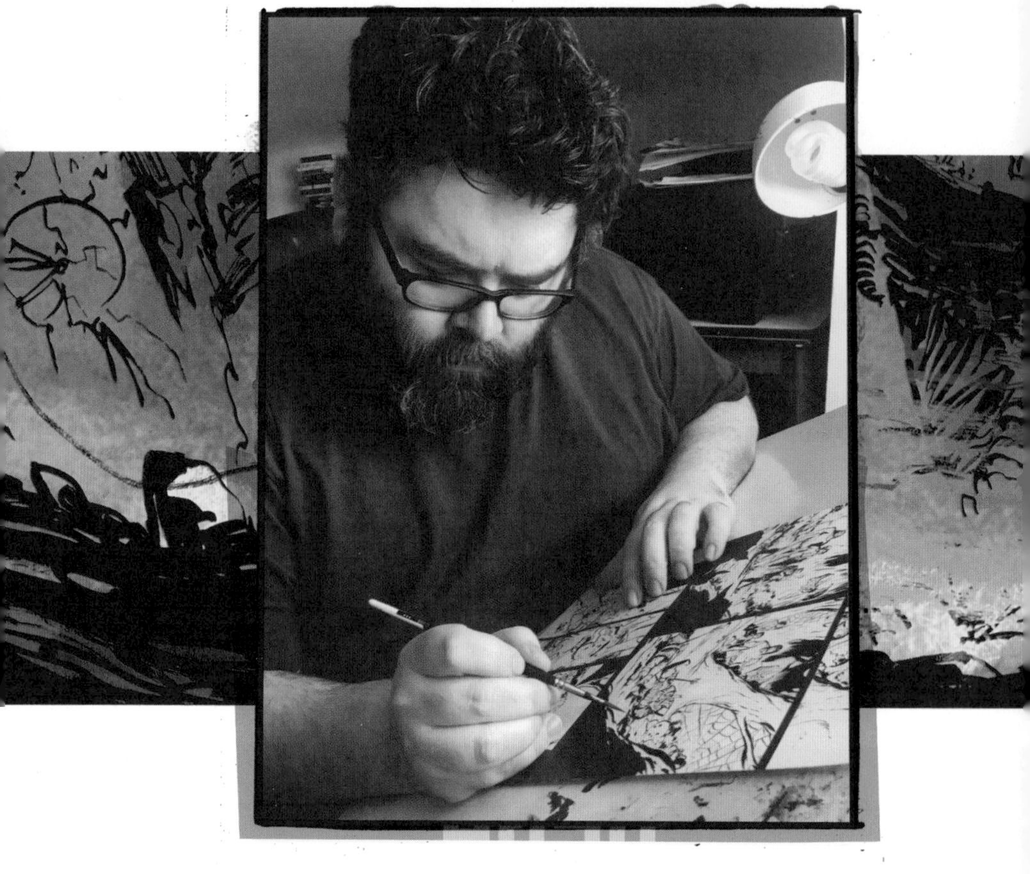

DAN MCDAID is a comics writer and artist from Scotland. Following a well-regarded run on the UK *Doctor Who* magazine, he cocreated the cosmic comedy drama *Jersey Gods* for Image Comics and the cult hit *Time Share* for Oni Press. Since then, he has worked on such properties as *Judge Dredd* and *Firefly*, codeveloped and drew TKO's *The Fearsome Doctor Fang*, and collaborated several times with fellow Scottish legend Irvine Welsh. He lives in a drafty old building overlooking the River Tay. *Dega* is his first graphic novel.